Contents

LIST OF BOX TITLES 6
ACKNOWLEDGMENTS 7
FOREWORD 9
INTRODUCTION 11
KEY MESSAGES 13

Part 1 - The Issue

THE EXTENT OF THE PROBLEM 19
- Youth homelessness defined 19
- Who are the young homeless 21
- Which areas have a youth homelessness problem 22
- How many young people 24
- Homelessness amongst under 18s 26
- Official statistics on youth homelessness 27

HOUSING OPTIONS FOR YOUNG PEOPLE 29
Low incomes 31
- unemployment 31
- benefits 34
- low pay 38

A shortage of suitable accommodation 39
- the private rented sector 39
- home ownership 41
- public housing 41

Failure of the Welfare Safety Nets 43
- Children Act 1989 43
- homelessness legislation 44
- community care 45

NO CHOICE BUT TO LEAVE 47
Unable to remain at home 49
- family conflict - a key factor 49
- are young people pushed or do they jump? 50
- families under pressure 51

Leaving home without support 54
Disadvantaged groups 56
care-leavers 56
young people from black and other ethnic minorities 58
young refugees and asylum seekers 60
young women 61
young lesbians and gay men 62

WHY WE SHOULD CARE 65
The effects on young people 66
little or no money 66
health problems 67
alcohol and drug misuse 69
anti-social behaviour and criminalisation 72
feelings of frustration and isolation 74
The high cost of youth homelessness 74

Part 2 - What we can do
SOMETHING CAN BE DONE 79

PREVENTION IS BETTER THAN CURE 81
Education 82
Advice 84
Preparation and support for young people leaving care 87
Increasing housing options 89
the private sector 89
the public and voluntary sectors 92
Increasing educational, training and employment opportunities 95
A benefit safety net 103
Family support 104
RECOMMENDATIONS 107

RESPONDING TO HOMELESSNESS 111
Assessing needs 113
Strengthening the safety nets 116
Providing accommodation, support and care 116
A range of different accommodation types 116
On-going and comprehensive support 120
RECOMMENDATIONS 125

"We don't choose to be homeless..."

Report of the National Inquiry into preventing Youth Homelessness

Written & researched by Angela Evans

LOCAL STRATEGIES . . . 127
Getting started . . . 129
Measuring needs . . . 131
Establishing a comprehensive strategy . . . 132
Developing links with other strategies . . . 134
Sharing information and good practice . . . 135
RECOMMENDATIONS . . . 136

A NATIONAL PRIORITY . . . 137
RECOMMENDATIONS . . . 138

REFERENCES . . . 139
By section . . . 139
Summary of main references . . . 148

APPENDICES . . . 149
Organisations submitting evidence . . . 149
Estimating the national incidence of youth homelessness . . . 153
Estimating the costs and benefits of reducing youth homelessness . . . 155
Case study contact details . . . 169
Summary of collaborating for success: organisational issues facing the youth homeless sector by McKinsey and company . . . 170

List of box titles

1. The aims of the inquiry
2. Organisations submitting evidence
3. A definition of youth homelessness
4. The extent of youth homelessness in 3 different locations
5. How many young people? - the views of local projects
6. How many young people? - some estimates from around the UK
7. Homelessness among the very young and vulnerable
8. A growing problem
9. The new poor
10. Unemployment rates by age group
11. The benefits gap
12. The strain of low beneft levels
13. Young people's earnings - 1995
14. Accommodation for young people in the private sector
15. Granting tenancies to 16/17 year olds
16. Social services departments' responsibilities to homeless 16/17 year olds under the children act 1989
17. Legislation - failing to meet the needs of homeless young people
18. Leaving home put in context
19. Family conflict and youth homelessness
20. Youth homelessness and abuse at home
21. Changing patterns of poverty
22. Youth homelessness and families under pressure
23. Rites of passage - contrasting transitions to independence
24. Homelessness among black and other ethnic minorities
25. Abdul's story (a 16 year old refugee)
26. Young women and homelessness
27. Nicky's story (the problems a gay 20 year old can face in finding suitable accommodation)
28. Youth unemployment: twice the national average
29. Increased mental health problems amongst young homeless people
30. Substance abuse and homelessness
31. Anti-social behaviour amongst young homeless people
32. Young homeless offenders
33. Education initiatives to prevent youth homelessness
34. Early advice and support to young people at risk of homelessness
35. Presenting advice to young people
36. Essential elements of a care plan
37. Key features of a through care strategy
38. Using the private sector
39. Using the public sector - newcastle city council furniture scheme
40. Andrew's story (an ex-offender who is hiv positive)
41. John's story (a community self-build participant)
42. Self help schemes
43. Malcolm's story (struggling with the benefits system)
44. Family mediation services
45. Sarah's story (from abuse to homelessness)
46. Providing a range of accommodation services to homeless young people
47. Sally's story (receiving the right support)
48. A comprehensive service to homeless young people
49. The chance to return to a supported environment
50. Kevin's story (receiving the right support)
51. Support with health issues
52. Support with moving into new accommodation
53. Support for substance misusers
54. Social opportunities and support
55. Centrepoint oxfordshire - a regional strategy on youth homelessness
56. Drawing up a comprehensive young persons' housing strategy
57. A strategy for young single people - South Ribble

Acknowledgments

The Inquiry has enjoyed the advice and support of a huge range of organisations and individuals and without any one of them the Inquiry would have been diminished.

THE INQUIRY WOULD LIKE TO THANK
All the organisations who, alongside their day to day work with homeless people, found time to submit evidence; the advisors and organisations that contributed to or commented on particular sections of the report; and all the organisations that have helped to promote the inquiry's work.

The **commissioning charities** who have supported the Inquiry in so many ways without dictating our agenda, represented by:
Steve Harwood (Barnardos), Ian Brady (Centrepoint), Jon Fitzmaurice (CHAR), Amanda Allard (The children's Society), Helen Dent (NCH Action For Children), Louise Casey (Shelter), Les Milner (St Basil's Birmingham), Sue Wald (Young Homelessness Group), Andrew Harris (YMCA), Geraldine Duddy (YWCA).

A particular thanks to:
Angela Evans - for researching and writing the report and the evidence working papers.
Keith Kemp - for coordinating the Inquiry secretariat.
Nick Brown - and the team at McKinsey for their working paper 'Collaborating for success: organisational issues facing the youth homelessness sector' and for their practical support.
Catherine Mattos - for researching and writing "Hearing Young People".
The Voices Group - all the young people in the voices group who contributed substantially to the report.
David Lewis and Penelope Rowlatt - for researching and developing the cost benefit analysis for the report.

and to:
Mary Ashman, Penny Cole, Russell Hains, Rebecca Grey, Helen Kay, Robert McFarlain, Mark Philips, Howard Rogers, Nigel Senior, Radiance Strathdee, Helen Taylor, Jenny Cantwell and all the staff at CHAR.

FUNDERS
The Inquiry is indebted to all those who provided resources both directly and in kind to enable the Inquiry to complete its work.

The financial contributions from: BET plc, Charity Projects, The Joseph Rowntree Foundation, Orbit Housing Association, Shell UK ltd. TSB foundation for England and Wales and John Laing plc.

Contributions in Kind from: Brunswick PR., Cardiff City Council, Coopers and Lybrand, The Halifax Building Society, McKinsey & Company, National Youth Agency, Institute of Housing.

Special thanks to the Joseph Rowntree Foundation who's initial support made the whole initiative possible.

Inquiry Members

Andreas Whittam-Smith (Chair): Founder and Editor of The Independent newspaper from 1986-1994 and Vice-President of the National Council for One Parent Families.

John Bird: Jointly founded "The Big Issue" in 1991 - currently the Editor

David Divine: Became the youngest ever Director of an English Social Services Department in 1986.

The Right Reverend Laurie Green: Bishop of Bradwell.

Diana Moore: Chair of the British Youth Council.

Professor Duncan Maclennan: Economic Advisor to the Joseph Rowntree Foundation and Director of their Housing Finance Program 1987-1991.

Bill Payne: Chief Executive Yorkshire Metropolitan Housing Association, President of the Chartered Institute of Housing and on the editorial board of ROOF magazine.

Dr Penelope Rowlatt: Director, National Economic Research Associates (NERA).

Earl Conrad Russell: Professor of British History at Kings College London, Liberal Democrat Spokesman on Social Security since 1990 and Treasurer of the All Party Committee on Homelessness.

Baden Skitt: Assistant Commissioner Metropolitan Police and a Director of the Educational Broadcasting Services Trust.

Vivienne Sugar: Chief Executive of the New Swansea Unitary Authority and previously Director of Housing for the City of Cardiff. She is a member of Joseph Rowntree's Housing Research Committee.

Wendy Thompson: Former Chief Executive of Turning Point, a charity for people with drink, drugs and mental health problems. Currently Chief Executive, London Borough of Newha.

Gordon Younger: Chief Executive of BACS Ltd.

Foreword

Andreas Whittam Smith, Chair of the Inquiry

Homelessness among young people virtually disappeared in the 1950s and 1960s and has since returned. The young homeless are the casualties of the journey everybody must make from dependence as a child to independence as an adult. This report provides a map of the pathways from dependence to independence and shows which routes still work and which have become hard going or nearly impossible.

Our Inquiry gains legitimacy, I believe, through being commissioned by 10 charities, each of which acts, in different ways, to mitigate homelessness among young people. We reflect the charities' concern that youth homelessness is widespread and relentlessly growing but is submerged, unrecorded and unnoticed. Instead of being called into existence by Government, this Inquiry is the result of voluntary initiative.

Were this a report for the Government our task would be finished. In due course, ministers would respond to the analysis and recommendations and decide what to do. I believe that there is a different sort of follow-up work to be done by our commissioning charities after this report has been read, considered and debated. I urge them to establish some sort of permanent body whose objective would be to carry forward as many of our recommendations as possible. I doubt whether a new organisation is needed. Even in the voluntary sector there can be too much bureaucracy. But a standing committee formed by our commissioners might answer the purpose. It is not enough to write a report and make proposals for improvement. Action must follow.

Introduction

Commissioned by ten leading charities, the Inquiry into Preventing Youth Homelessness was established in mid-1995 to take a fresh look at the issue of homelessness amongst young people and make recommendations for preventative and remedial action.

Inquiry members were drawn from a range of different backgrounds, including housing, social services, the police, the Church and business. Young people with experience of homelessness were also directly involved in the process.

figure 1
THE AIMS OF THE INQUIRY WERE:

1. To outline the causes and scale of youth homelessness.
2. To identify the major problems facing young people entering the housing market.
3. To identify solutions to youth homelessness that are effective and affordable.
4. To give priority to the issue of youth homelessness.

THE INQUIRY GATHERED INFORMATION IN A NUMBER OF WAYS:

1. An open invitation to submit evidence produced submissions from 170 organisations, including local authorities, housing associations, national voluntary organisations and local voluntary groups (A full list of those submitting evidence is included at Appendix 1).
2. A wide range of published research and data was considered and analysed.
3. Research was commissioned to explore the views of young homeless people on their experiences, the services available, and what other action should be taken.
4. A group of young people from homeless projects run by some of the commissioning charities were brought together to input directly into the inquiry process. This became known as the Voices group.
5. Working papers on the organisation and efficiency of the sector and the cost implications of youth homelessness were presented to the inquiry by, amongst others, McKinsey & Company.
6. Inquiry members made personal visits to projects working with young homeless people.

Inquiry members believe they have undertaken the most thorough and extensive examination of youth homelessness this century and that the report's recommendations, if implemented, would dramatically reduce the number of young homeless people.

figure2
ORGANISATIONS SUBMITTING EVIDENCE

	No.	%
National voluntary organisations	43	25
Other national organisations	4	2
Local voluntary groups	58	34
Local authorities	25	15
Housing associations	10	6
Local housing forums	11	6
Academic institutions	6	4
Others	13	8
Total	**170**	**100**

THE REPORT

1. The report presents the inquiry's main findings and recommendations on youth homelessness. It refers extensively to the evidence received by the inquiry, and draws on many other published sources.
2. As well as providing an analysis of the problem, the report outlines in some detail the different ways in which the circumstances and prospects of young people can be improved.
3. Part 1 of the report provides an analysis of the extent, causes and consequences of youth homelessness. Part 2 demonstrates what can be done to prevent and respond to youth homelessness by describing a range of innovative and effective local projects and policies and making detailed recommendations for action.
4. The key messages of the report are summarised overleaf. Unless otherwise stated, evidence quoted has been submitted to the inquiry.

Key messages

HOMELESSNESS AMONGST YOUNG PEOPLE

...IS A LARGE AND GROWING PROBLEM

(Part 1, The extent of the problem)

Homelessness can and does touch the lives of 'ordinary' young people and their families.

In 1995 at least 246,000 young people became homeless in the United Kingdom estimates the inquiry.

The problem has grown at an alarming rate over recent years and local agencies are finding it difficult to cope.

Youth homelessness is not a marginal social problem, affecting only a small number of disaffected young people sleeping rough in London or other big cities.

Young people are homeless in every part of the country - in rural as well as urban locations, the north as well as the south and in affluent as well as depressed areas.

The majority of young homeless people are not sleeping rough, but are hidden away in a range of temporary housing situations - for example, living in a hostel or bed and breakfast hotel, or over-staying their welcome with friends or relatives.

Young homeless people vary widely in terms of their backgrounds, circumstances, prospects and hopes. A common misconception is that young homeless people are all social misfits, living on the margins of society, embroiled in an underworld of drugs, petty crime and prostitution. In reality: some have comfortable family backgrounds while others have experienced poverty, neglect and abuse; some are in full time education while others are poorly educated and trained; some will experience homelessness as a temporary crisis whilst for others it will be a recurring problem.

...IS CAUSED BY A RANGE OF SOCIAL AND ECONOMIC FACTORS

(Part 1, Housing options for young people)

Youth unemployment, low wages, reduced benefit rates, a shortage of affordable housing and limited access to public housing have all contributed to the problem of youth homelessness.

Young people have borne the brunt of changes in patterns of employment, such as the decline in demand for unskilled labour and the increase in part-time and temporary employment. Rather than soften the blow of these developments, government policies have actually exacerbated the situation for many young people.

Welfare benefits to young people have been substantially reduced on the grounds that those unable to support themselves should rely on their families for help. However, in a contradictory move, the government has also cut the benefits payable to the parents of young people making it more difficult for family members to support each other.

...IS PARTICULARLY WIDESPREAD WITHIN CERTAIN DISADVANTAGED GROUPS

(Part 1, No choice but to leave)

A growing minority of homeless people are very young with multiple problems and needs. They are usually sleeping rough or living in hostels or bed and breakfast hotels, are no older than 18 and sometimes considerably younger, and many have been in care or have been abused or neglected by their families.

Young women, black and ethnic minority people and lesbians and gay men are more vulnerable to homelessness because they are more likely than other young people to be socially and economically disadvantaged.

...REPRESENTS A FAILURE OF A NORMAL PROCESS

(Part 1, No choice but to leave)

Leaving home is part of the journey from dependence to independence that all young people expect to make between the ages of 16 and 25.

Traditional pathways to independence have disappeared or become blocked for increasing numbers of young people. In the past, employment, education or marriage provided the resources and the legitimacy to leave the family home. Now, employment and housing opportunities are more limited and low wages and benefits for young people do not easily support independent living. As a consequence a larger proportion of young people are living with their parents, and those who have no option but to leave are more likely to find themselves homeless or in poor quality, insecure accommodation.

...IS LESS LIKELY TO HAPPEN WHEN THE TRANSITION TO INDEPENDENCE IS GRADUAL AND SUPPORTED

(Part 1, No choice but to leave)

Young people who are unsupported and unprepared when they leave home and who do not have the opportunity of returning during difficult times, are at a much greater risk of becoming homeless. Support is critically important to a successful transition to independence.

Most people receive a variety of formal and informal support during this period. For example, emotional and financial support from their parents, the opportunity to return home if things do not work out or accommodation provided by either an employer or an educational institution.

...HOMELESSNESS AMONGST YOUNG PEOPLE IS NOT THE FAULT OF YOUNG PEOPLE

(Part 1, No choice but to leave)

Most young homeless people have left home because they have had to or because being homeless is preferable to being badly treated and abused at home. Youth homelessness is not the product of fecklessness or wanting too much too soon. Changing family relationships and structures, financial pressures and poor housing conditions have increased tensions at home, sometimes to the point where a young person has no option but to leave. The outcome for many young people is homelessness, especially if they are unsupported by the limited safety nets provided by the welfare state.

...WILL BE MUCH MORE DIFFICULT TO PUT RIGHT IN FUTURE IF WE DO NOTHING NOW

(Part 1, Why we should care)

The human and financial costs of turning a blind eye to the problems of youth homelessness are considerable. The experience can have a devastating and lasting effect on a young person. Young homeless people are not only without a home - they are usually without a job, have no or very little income, poor health and low self esteem.

It is cheaper and more humane to respond rapidly and positively to the needs of young people than to respond only when those needs have multiplied, become problematic and require crisis intervention in the form, for example, of specialist care and extra policing.

A young person once homeless becomes a problem and the need for housing becomes a need for rehabilitation. The longer homelessness continues the more likely it is that young people will become involved in drugs, heavy drinking, petty crime and prostitution and that their physical and mental health will deteriorate.

It may be more expensive to allow a young person to fall through the safety net and end up homeless than to provide the support they need to make the transition to independence. This was one of key conclusions of a cost benefit analysis commissioned by the inquiry.(see appendix 3). And it refers to purely financial savings taking no account of the considerable human costs that homelessness imposes upon young people and the wider community.

...REQUIRES A RANGE OF DIFFERENT SOLUTIONS

(Part 2)

Just as there is no single cause of youth homelessness, there is no single solution.

Homelessness amongst young people is the consequence of a wide array of different factors and like the rest of the population young homeless people have diverse needs and preferences. It is, therefore, essential that our responses are comprehensive and coordinated.

Local and national agencies need to work closely together to make the best use of resources and energies and to ensure that young people do not fall through the safety nets that are in place to catch them.

Every area should have a local strategy providing both a spur to action and a framework for the many different types of initiatives described in this report.

In addition to these key messages there are recommendations at the end of each section of part 2 - What we can do. These recommendations strongly suggest that whilst there is no single solution to the problem of youth homelessness a great deal could be done to greatly reduce the problem. And much of it need not cost a great deal.

PART 1

THE ISSUE

1 THE EXTENT OF THE PROBLEM

2 HOUSING OPTIONS FOR YOUNG PEOPLE

3 NO CHOICE BUT TO LEAVE

4 WHY WE SHOULD CARE

PART 1

The extent of the problem

It is important that we measure the incidence of homelessness amongst young people. Local evidence is revealing and useful, but we need to know more about the national picture if the issue is to receive the profile and priority it deserves.

Only by measuring the full extent of youth homelessness can we ascertain whether policies and initiatives aimed at tackling the problem are effective.

In this section we examine available evidence on the incidence of youth homelessness and, in the absence of any official national figure, the inquiry presents an estimate of the extent of the problem.

YOUTH HOMELESSNESS DEFINED

It is often assumed that all or most young homeless people are sleeping rough. In fact, **only a minority of young homeless people are literally without a roof over their head at any one point in time.**

Local survey findings, submitted to the inquiry as evidence, suggest that around a tenth of young homeless people are sleeping rough when they approach a housing or advice agency for help.1 Unfortunately, many of the other housing situations that young people find themselves in, such as bed and breakfast hotels, hostels or squatting, can be just as unsuitable and traumatic.

Many of these housing situations are precarious and in the absence of decent alternatives **young people frequently move from one place to another caught in a depressing cycle of unsuitable, stop-gap living arrangements.** The use of stock or snapshot figures fails, therefore, to provide accurate estimates of the scale of youth homelessness today *(see How many young people, page 24)*.

The inquiry definition of youth homelessness includes a number of unsatisfactory temporary housing situations (figure 3) since it is clearly not just those young people who are on the streets at any one point in time who are without a home.

The inclusion of a range of different housing situations is important if we are to get a representative picture of youth homelessness. Women, black and other ethnic minority people and lesbians and gay men, are much more likely to be staying with relatives or friends, for example, than sleeping rough.[2]

A survey of homeless young people conducted in 1995 found that about half of black and Asian young people had stayed with relatives and friends before entering a hostel, compared with just a quarter of young white people, and that sleeping rough was viewed as a 'last resort' by black and Asian young people.[3]

Young homeless people in rural areas also appear to be less likely to sleep rough than those in urban areas.[4] Focusing exclusively on the 'sharp end' of homelessness - sleeping rough - is therefore likely to produce an incomplete and misleading impression of the problem, leading to solutions that are crisis orientated and aimed at picking up the pieces rather than preventing homeless situations developing in the first place.

Whilst homeless, the majority stay with friends and relations, often moving from one place to another. Many live in this unsettled way for months, even years. Education and job opportunities are severely limited to those living in such unsettled circumstances. This sort of homelessness goes unrecognised, and yet is a large problem for young single people who are forced to leave home.
Hackney Youth Unemployment Project.

The inquiry definition of youth homelessness excludes young people who are living with their parents or in their own accommodation but want or need to move. This is because these young people do have a home and in some cases problems can be resolved without the young person having to move out. However, this is not to say that the needs of these groups should be overlooked. Early intervention in such cases can prevent future hardship and possible homelessness.

In some cases it is impossible or undesirable for a young person to remain where they are (for example, where there has been an irretrievable breakdown in family relations or where there has been abuse). In these circumstances agencies should provide suitable alternative accommodation as quickly as possible. (see Part 2, *What We Can Do*).

figure 3

A DEFINITION OF YOUTH HOMELESSNESS

A single person, without dependants, between the ages of 16 and 25 years who is in one of the following housing situations:

1. without any accommodation - for example, sleeping rough or with no accommodation to go to;
2. in temporary accommodation such as a hostel, bed and breakfast hotel, squat;
3. staying temporarily with friends or relatives, who are unable/unwilling to accommodate in the longer term.

WHO ARE THE YOUNG HOMELESS

The belief that young homeless people are different to other young people is common place. They are often viewed as social misfits living on the margins of society and embroiled in an underworld of drugs, petty crime and prostitution.

Explanations of the problem tend to be diverse - ranging from a belief that young homeless people are irresponsible and create their own housing problems, to the view that youth homelessness is the product of poor parenting and a deprived background.

Although precise definitions may vary, youth homelessness is generally perceived as a marginal social problem affecting only a small minority. The assumption that the problem is concentrated in large cities, in particular London, keeps the issue comfortingly remote and sustains the belief that homelessness rarely touches the lives of ordinary young people and their families.

Young homeless people in fact come from a surprisingly wide variety of backgrounds.
A survey conducted in 1996 by the St Mungo Association in London found that almost a half of its residents in hostels, care homes and halfway houses had academic qualifications - a quarter had O levels or GCSEs, one in ten was educated to A level standard and a further tenth had a degree.[5]

Just like the rest of the population, young homeless people have diverse backgrounds, circumstances, prospects and hopes. Some young homeless people have comfortable family backgrounds, while others have experienced poverty, neglect and abuse; some are in full time education while others are poorly educated and trained; for some homelessness is a temporary crisis whilst for others it is a recurring problem.

Reductions in welfare benefits, unemployment, changing family relations and structures and a shortage of suitable accommodation have affected the lives of young people across the social spectrum.
There is, however, consistent evidence that **certain groups, such as women and young people from black and other ethnic minorities, experience these problems more acutely and are, as a consequence, more vulnerable to homelessness.** For example, a Department of the

Environment survey undertaken in 1992/93 found that a quarter of all homeless applicants to nine local authorities in England were black, Asian or from some other ethnic minority, although in 1991 people from ethnic minorities represented just 6% of the population.[6]

Surveys in London have shown that more than half of young homeless people are black or from other ethnic minorities, although they make up only 20% of the local population.[7] The incidence of homelessness amongst disadvantaged groups is discussed in more detail in Section 3 - No choice but to leave.

WHICH AREAS HAVE A YOUTH HOMELESSNESS PROBLEM?

There is a significant problem of youth homelessness in Richmond upon Thames. This may not be expected in an apparently wealthy borough, but the high cost of housing and the resulting shortage of affordable accommodation makes it difficult for people to meet their housing needs.

London Borough of Richmond upon Thames

Youth homelessness is not just a 'London' or 'big city' phenomenon. Around 80% of local submissions to the inquiry came from outside London (see Appendix 1) and, regardless of area type, all described a widespread and growing problem.

Affluent and depressed, rural and urban, northern and southern - all areas have been affected by the economic, social and political forces that have contributed to the problem of youth homelessness. Local surveys repeatedly demonstrate that homelessness is overwhelmingly local in nature, affecting indigenous young people who want to continue living locally.

A snapshot from the dozens of local homeless surveys submitted to the inquiry highlights the geographical spread (figure 4). The inquiry shows clearly that **the problem of youth homelessness is widespread, on the increase and affecting a wide range of young people.**

Homelessness and housing problems are experienced by young people from a variety of backgrounds throughout the United Kingdom. What they all have in common is a need for decent, affordable and safe accommodation.

figure 4

THE EXTENT OF YOUTH HOMELESSNESS IN 3 DIFFERENT LOCATIONS

CARDIFF

A multi-agency survey undertaken in Cardiff over a six-month period during 1993/94 found 324 young people between the ages of 16 and 21 who were either homeless or in serious housing need. This represents almost a quarter of all applicants accepted as statutorily homeless by Cardiff City Council over that period.

Disturbingly, 56% of these young people were just 16 or 17 years of age. The multi-agency working group which conducted the survey concluded: *'The priority is the 16 to 17 year old age group, in particular young women. A significant proportion of this most vulnerable group slept rough during the survey period and the vast majority were seeking a more or less permanent solution to their accommodation problems. This is a significant challenge to the housing agencies involved since current Government policy is based on the philosophy that 16/17-year olds should remain at home with their families.'*

Survey of young people presenting as homeless in Cardiff, October '93 to March '94: Multi-Agency Working Group on Youth Homelessness

OLDHAM

A 1995 survey in Oldham of over 200 young people aged 16 to 25 found that almost a half (45%) had experienced homelessness. This proportion is surprisingly high given that the survey was broadly based and included young people approaching a range of different agencies such as a local college, a Citizens' Advice Bureau and the local employment service. The survey report concluded: *'Homelessness amongst young people is a serious issue that needs to be addressed. The high numbers of respondents stating that they have been homeless and the long periods involved are both causes for concern.'*

Key to the door: the housing needs and aspirations of young people in Oldham, August '95.

GLOUCESTERSHIRE

A survey of young homeless people, undertaken in 1994 by Gloucestershire Forum for Young Single Homelessness, found 1,148 young people within the county who were homeless or in housing need. This compares with around 930 homeless households accepted for rehousing over the same period.

The survey also found that the proportion of young women and 16/17-year olds who were homeless had increased since the year before - in 1994 women represented 40% of all young homeless people compared with 32% in 1993, and the proportion aged under 18 increased from 22% to 33% over the same period.

Finding the right combination: a report on young people's housing needs and provision in Gloucestershire 1994-1995, Gloucestershire Forum for Young Single People, 1995.

HOW MANY YOUNG PEOPLE

There is no official national measure of youth homelessness because young people without dependants have very few rights to housing and many local authorities do not, therefore, keep a record of their needs (see *Official Statistics on youth homelessness - page 27*).

The inquiry has calculated that at least 246,000 young people in the United Kingdom were homeless in 1995. This means that around one in thirty people between the ages of 16 and 25 became homeless during 1995. Over a longer period, the proportion of young people who have experienced homelessness is clearly higher. The number of young people who were homeless in 1995 exceeds the number of households accepted as homeless by UK local authorities over the same period by some 50% (Appendix 2 describes the method of calculation used).

figure 5

HOW MANY YOUNG PEOPLE? - THE VIEWS OF LOCAL PROJECTS

No central data-base exists in Strathclyde to collate the information obtained by the various agencies involved in tackling youth homelessness...It is therefore difficult to establish the pattern of homelessness and recurring homelessness. However, it is clear from available information that the scale of youth homelessness is unprecedented, and this trend shows no sign of abating.

Strathclyde Regional Council

There is widespread recognition of a growing gap between housing and service needs for single people in Stevenage and the resources to meet those needs. The situation is more acute for young single people than for any other group.

Stevenage Borough Council

A particularly serious problem has been emerging in Northern Ireland over the past few years - that is, the problem of homelessness amongst young single people.

Northern Ireland Council for the Homeless

There is no doubt that homelessness amongst young people has increased dramatically over recent years, especially amongst the youngest and most vulnerable. Available statistics confirm this trend, as do the testimonies of the large number of organisations dealing with the problem on a daily basis many of whom submitted evidence to the inquiry.

figure 6

HOW MANY YOUNG PEOPLE? - SOME ESTIMATES FROM AROUND THE UK

- **Around a quarter** of single homeless people sleeping rough or living in hostels or bed and breakfast hotels are under 25 years of age.[10]
- Single 16 to 25 year olds account for **around a quarter** of all homeless applications to local authorities in the UK - this does not include those who are pregnant.[11]
- Almost 6,000 single homeless people were referred to Stonham Housing Association during the first six months of 1995 and **over half** (55%) of these were under 25 years of age.[12]
- **Almost half** of the 99 homeless people identified by a Swansea Cyrenians outreach service in outlying areas of Swansea during 1995 were under 25 years of age.[13]
- **Over two-thirds** (69%) of homeless people who approached a housing advice service in Bradford during 1994/95 were under 25 years of age.[14]
- **Over half** (54%) of the inquiries received during 1995 by London-based Homeless Action were from or concerning women under 25 years of age.[15]
- The Scottish Young Person's Survey found that **6% of young people who had left home by the age of 19** had experienced periods of homelessness. This is likely to under estimate the extent of the problem since young homeless people will have been more difficult to locate for the survey.[16]

Homelessness amongst young people is a major problem. Young people between the ages of 16 and 25 account for 17% of the total adult (16+) population, yet they form a much larger proportion of homeless people.

Not only are young people more likely than older people to become homeless, but **homelessness amongst young people is growing at a faster rate than for any other group.** Local trend data submitted as evidence to the inquiry builds up to a national picture of a growing problem that local agencies are struggling to cope with.

figure 7

A GROWING PROBLEM

- A hostel for single homeless people in Taunton reports a **three-fold increase** in the past three years in the number of 16 to 25-year olds using the hostel.[17]
- A youth centre in South Wales reports that in 1995 almost a third (30%) of their clients were homeless, compared with 17% in 1990.[18]
- A project for young homeless people in Glasgow reports that in the first six months of 1995/96 they have seen almost as many young people as in the whole of 1994/95.[19]

- Swansea Cyrenians experienced a **40% increase** in the number of inquiries from homeless people under the age of 25 during 1995.[20]
- In September 1989 only 4% of those who used St Annes, a voluntary sector project for single homeless people in Leeds, were under 25 years of age. The same age group now makes up 37% of all those who approach and use the centre.[21]

HOMELESSNESS AMONGST UNDER 18s

The greatest increase in homelessness seems to have occurred amongst the very young and vulnerable. Centrepoint recently conducted research in London and six other locations in England and Northern Ireland involving interviews with over 7,500 homeless young people: they found that growing numbers of *'highly vulnerable, very young people'* were becoming homeless.[8]

The charity estimates that four in ten young people on the streets today ran away from home or care before they were 16 years of age.[9] Evidence submitted to the inquiry confirms this picture.

figure 8
HOMELESSNESS AMONG THE VERY YOUNG AND VULNERABLE

- **66%** of the young people seen by the Young Single Homeless Project in Portsmouth in 1994 were **under 18 years of age,** a 54% increase on the previous year and the biggest increase for any group;
- There was almost a **three-fold increase** in the number of vulnerable young people accepted as homeless by Leeds City Council between 1990/91 and 1994/95;
- Stopover, a voluntary organisation which manages direct access and other accommodation for 16 to 21-year olds in the London Borough of Lewisham has found that the percentage of 16/17-year olds has increased from around 30% to 50% of the total intake over the past two years;
- Hove YMCA reports that it has seen an increase in the proportion of clients who are under 18 years, with around 60% of enquiries in 1995 coming from this group.

Homeless 16/17-year olds often have multiple problems and needs (see section 4 *Why We Should Care*). Most have left home early, usually following abuse or neglect, or have been in local authority care, and many end up sleeping rough or living in bed and breakfast hotels or squats.

With no home, little or no income and no-one to protect them, the very young are often at the 'sharp end' of homelessness and in need of urgent help. We should not, however, base our understanding of youth homelessness, nor our responses, simply on the acute realities experienced by this group.

OFFICIAL STATISTICS ON YOUTH HOMELESSNESS

Official statistics seem to turn a blind eye to young homeless people. **The great majority of young people are not eligible for public housing** and so, understandably, do not apply for help - those who do apply often go unrecorded.

Young homeless people who do not have children and are not pregnant must usually be defined as 'vulnerable' and in 'priority need' in order to be rehoused under the homelessness legislation.[22] **Very few local authorities define young homeless people as vulnerable on the basis of age alone[23] and so the majority of young applicants are rejected.**

Since official homelessness statistics focus on those who have applied and been accepted for rehousing under the legislation,[24] they inevitably under-represent young people.

A 1991 Department of the Environment study of single homeless people found that only about two-fifths of those under 25 years of age had applied to a council as homeless.[25] Other surveys put the proportion who apply even lower - for example, a survey of single people approaching housing advice agencies in London during June 1992 found that less than a tenth (8%) had applied to a council in the past 12 months.[26]

Similarly, social service departments are only likely to record young homeless people if they believe that they may be eligible for assistance under the Children Act 1989 or the NHS and Community Care Act 1993. Young homeless people are not generally considered a priority group for welfare services, and **many social service authorities would not normally assist a young homeless person unless they had a problem additional to their lack of housing, such as mental illness or a disability.**[27]

Even for 16/17-year olds, who fall within the provisions of the Children Act, homelessness alone is usually not sufficient to gain access to housing. Given that the majority of young homeless people fall outside the social services safety net, social service statistics cannot provide a reliable measure of the problem. A study of single homelessness in Hampshire, for example, found that only two out of 13 authorities recorded fully each referral under the Children Act and its outcome.[28]

National housing-needs assessments are undertaken regularly by the Department of the Environment and other national housing bodies in order to estimate the number of additional dwellings that are required to meet national housing needs. The figures generated by these assessments, and the methods they employ, have been the subject of some debate over recent years.

The Environment Select Committee recently conducted an inquiry into national housing needs and the Department of the Environment, for the first time in 20 years, has made public its own housing needs projections. However, it seems very unlikely that this renewal of interest in housing-needs assessments will generate a national estimate of youth homelessness.

Young single people are under-counted or excluded entirely from national housing-needs assessments on the grounds that *'there is no consensus about them having a legitimate expectation of access to subsidised housing.'* [29]

However, this exclusion is rarely made explicit and the complex methods used to derive estimates often disguise any underlying value judgements. As a consequence, the systematic exclusion and under-counting of young single people is rarely highlighted or criticised.

In its report on housing needs, the Environment Select Committee expressed concern at the exclusion of single people from needs assessments and advised that *'care should be taken to ensure that covert moral judgements should not enter considerations of need when it comes to such a basic human requirement as shelter.'* [30]

PART 1

Housing options for young people

Leaving home is a part of the transition that young people make from childhood to adulthood, dependence to independence. Over recent years, however, this journey to independence has become increasingly hazardous and as a consequence young people have become more vulnerable to homelessness.

The normal process of leaving home has become fraught with difficulty and danger. The traditional and acceptable pathways to independence, such as employment and education, appear to have become harder to follow for a large and growing number of young people.

High unemployment and low pay and reduced benefit levels mean that young people often have insufficient purchasing power in the private sector and, except in special circumstances, do not qualify for public housing. Many young people therefore have few housing options available to them when they leave the parental home.

The biggest constraint on choice is lack of money. Youth unemployment has risen over recent years and the reduced benefit rates that are paid to young people do not readily support a young person living independently.

Even employment is not the reliable route to independence it used to be. Wages amongst young people are low and have dropped as a proportion of average wages over recent years. Young single people today are much more likely to experience unemployment and poverty.

Figure 9 shows that in 1979 single people and childless couples below pensionable age accounted for just a fifth (19%) of the poorest 10% of households. In 1992/93 this proportion had risen sharply to over a third (34%). In contrast, the proportion of pensioner households actually dropped over the same period, and the proportion of households with children rose by just a few percent.

This strongly suggests that we need to reappraise our perceptions of poverty and our assumptions about the types of household who are most likely to be affected.

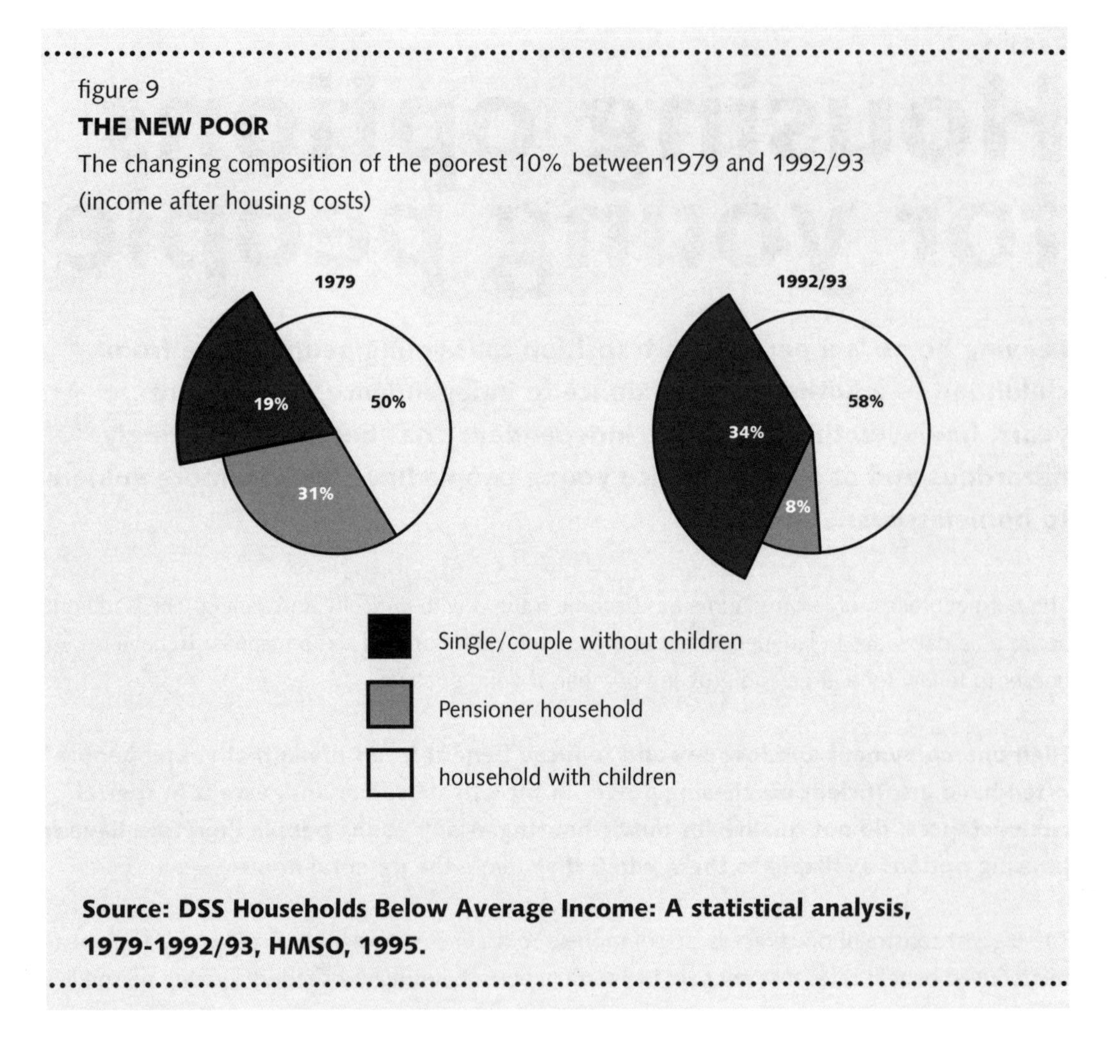

To compound the difficulties experienced by young people, the pool of affordable accommodation available to them has contracted - most owner-occupied and private rented accommodation is out of their financial reach and young people are not considered a priority for public housing.

Young people across the social spectrum experience difficulties finding suitable, affordable accommodation: some groups, such as black and Asian young people (see page 58) and young people leaving care (see page 56) are especially disadvantaged.

As a consequence of these multiple difficulties many young people have little choice but to continue living with their parents. This restriction on mobility reduces the efficiency of the labour market and further limits the ability of young people to find work.

LOW INCOMES

UNEMPLOYMENT

Employment is the only means to escape poverty. Employment is crucial in establishing a positive focus in life, improving quality of life by broadening financial capabilities, heightening a sense of worth, value and esteem. A young person has the right to expect opportunities, yet the image portrayed by the media is one of the undeserving poor, scroungers and a burden on society, all of which increases the feeling of alienation and maintains low expectations.
St Anne's Centre, Leeds

Employment is critically important in effecting the transition to adulthood, providing not just the resources for a young person to be able to live away from home but also conferring adult status. Unfortunately, young people have borne the brunt of the economic recession and are far more likely to be unemployed than any other group in the work force.

In Spring 1996, the unemployment rate for 16 to 24-year olds was around 15% (see figure 10), roughly twice the national average.[1] This gap between the unemployment rates of young people and the population as a whole has widened over recent years - in 1992 the youth unemployment rate was 67% higher than the national average, in 1995 it was 81% higher. In October 1995, young people between the ages of 18 and 24 accounted for over a quarter (27%) of all unemployed people.[2]

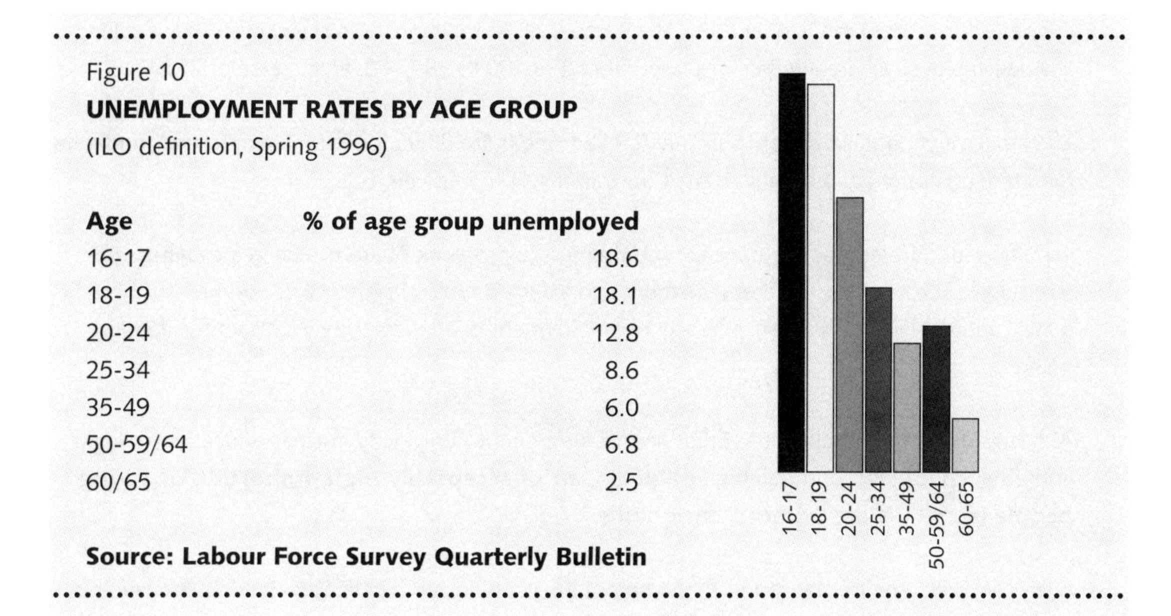
Figure 10
UNEMPLOYMENT RATES BY AGE GROUP
(ILO definition, Spring 1996)

Age	% of age group unemployed
16-17	18.6
18-19	18.1
20-24	12.8
25-34	8.6
35-49	6.0
50-59/64	6.8
60/65	2.5

Source: Labour Force Survey Quarterly Bulletin

The true unemployment rate for young people is likely to be significantly higher since official statistics include only those who are unemployed and receiving benefits. Government figures exclude 16/17-year olds since only in very limited circumstances can they claim benefits other than a Youth Training Scheme Allowance.

The Low Pay Unit estimates that in 1995 there were 750,000 young people in the United Kingdom between the ages of 16 and 24 who were unemployed, not on a Youth Training Scheme or in education and not claiming benefit.[3] If these young people were included in official statistics the unemployment rate for young people would almost double.

Official figures also disguise the dramatic variations between different areas and groups. Unemployment rates at the regional level varied by as much as six percentage points in 1995, from 11.8% in Northern Ireland to 6.4% in East Anglia.[4] But even these regional differences mask the way in which unemployment is concentrated in particular areas and groups.

In some inner-city areas and on some housing estates, the great majority of young people are out of work and unemployment is viewed as almost a natural and unalterable condition. The unemployment rate amongst black and other ethnic minority young people is alarmingly high. For example, in Spring 1994, 33% of 16 to 24-year olds from black and other ethnic minority groups were unemployed, compared to 15% of white men and women.[5] Young black men and women have extremely high rates of unemployment - 47% of African-Caribbean young people were unemployed in 1995.[5]

The fact that young people represent a growing proportion of the long-term unemployed (i.e. those out of work for more than 12 months) also indicates that **for many young people unemployment is not just a passing problem - an inevitable gap between leaving school or college and finding a job - but is a much more lasting feature of their lives.** Over the period October 1990 to October 1995, the number of 16 to 24-year old claimants who were long-term unemployed in Great Britain increased from 473,100 to 589,800, an increase of 25%.[6]

The longer a young person remains unemployed, the more difficult it is for them to find work and the more disillusioned and disheartened they are likely to become.

A number of different factors have contributed to the problem. There has been a decline in the traditional sources of unskilled employment and young people are often without the qualifications, skills or experience to secure employment in an increasingly competitive labour market.

Although increased numbers of young people are going to university, further-education colleges and other educational and training institutions, **an unacceptably high proportion of young people in the UK are without basic skills**.[7]

The Basic Skills Agency has found that a half of 16-year olds in the UK have inadequate levels of literacy[8] and employers have warned that a worryingly high proportion of the young people they see are unemployable because they lack the foundation skills required for vocational training[9]
In spite of the Government's stated commitment to youth training, **there are now widely held concerns that Youth Training (YT) programmes are failing very many young people.**

The proportion of young people entering YT courses has dropped significantly over recent years - for example, in 1994 just 12% of those who had finished compulsory education entered YT, compared with 21% in 1989.[10] Furthermore, nearly half (44%) of those who enrol for YT drop out before the end of the course and for young black trainees the proportion rises to two-thirds.[11]

There is widespread concern over the quality of training provided. In particular, the Government's emphasis on output-related funding has meant that training providers have concentrated on selecting those trainees most likely to succeed and those requiring more intensive training, including the homeless, find that the right support is unavailable.[12]

The Dearing Report, commissioned by the Government in 1995 to evaluate the framework of qualifications for 16 to 19-year olds, also expresses concern over the disappointing record and tarnished image of Youth Training.[13] There are fears that Modern Apprenticeships, introduced in 1995 to complement Youth Training, will attract the most able young people, further damaging the standing of YT schemes.

The difficulties young unemployed people experience finding suitable housing can also make it impossible for them to move in search of work. A CBI survey has found that over a third of unemployed 16 to 24-year olds think that a shortage of local jobs and an 'inability to relocate' are major barriers to them acquiring employment.[14]

Years ago, it was fairly common for employers to provide housing for their apprentices and young workers - at one time Barclays and National Westminster banks had several hundred hostel bedspaces in London for their staff - nowadays this sort of provision is rare, tying young people to the parental home and making it even more difficult for them to move in search of work.

The restrictions unemployment places on young people's ability to take responsibility are compounded by a benefit system which provides a threadbare safety net instead of a passport to independence.

If unemployment and enforced dependency continue for any length of time they can create a permanent condition of exclusion.

A recent Department for Education and Employment report revealed that a growing number of young people, about 12% of their age group, leave school without qualifications and lack even the most basic skills needed to enter the labour market.

The report says that these young people have *'low self-worth, little pride in their community, no hope for the future and feelings of rejection'* and that *'disaffection amongst young people serves to delay their transition to adulthood.'*[15]

BENEFITS

The inquiry members are in no doubt that the reduction in benefits to young people under the age of 25 years has dramatically increased the number who are homeless and in housing need. Not all young people are able to remain with their families until they are 25-years old and, with benefit rates as they currently stand, it is almost impossible for the unemployed to secure suitable alternative accommodation.

Since 1988, 16/17-year olds have only been able to claim benefit in very exceptional circumstances. If unemployed they are expected to attend a Youth Training Scheme for which they are paid a training allowance of £29.50 for 16-year olds and £35 for 17-year olds. These rates have remained constant since 1989 and 1986 respectively, and figure 11 shows that they represent only a quarter of a 'modest but adequate' weekly budget for a single person (excluding housing costs).[16]

If living independently, 16/17-year olds may be able to claim a discretionary hardship payment but these are difficult to obtain and are only awarded for a few weeks at a time.[17]

figure 11
THE BENEFITS GAP

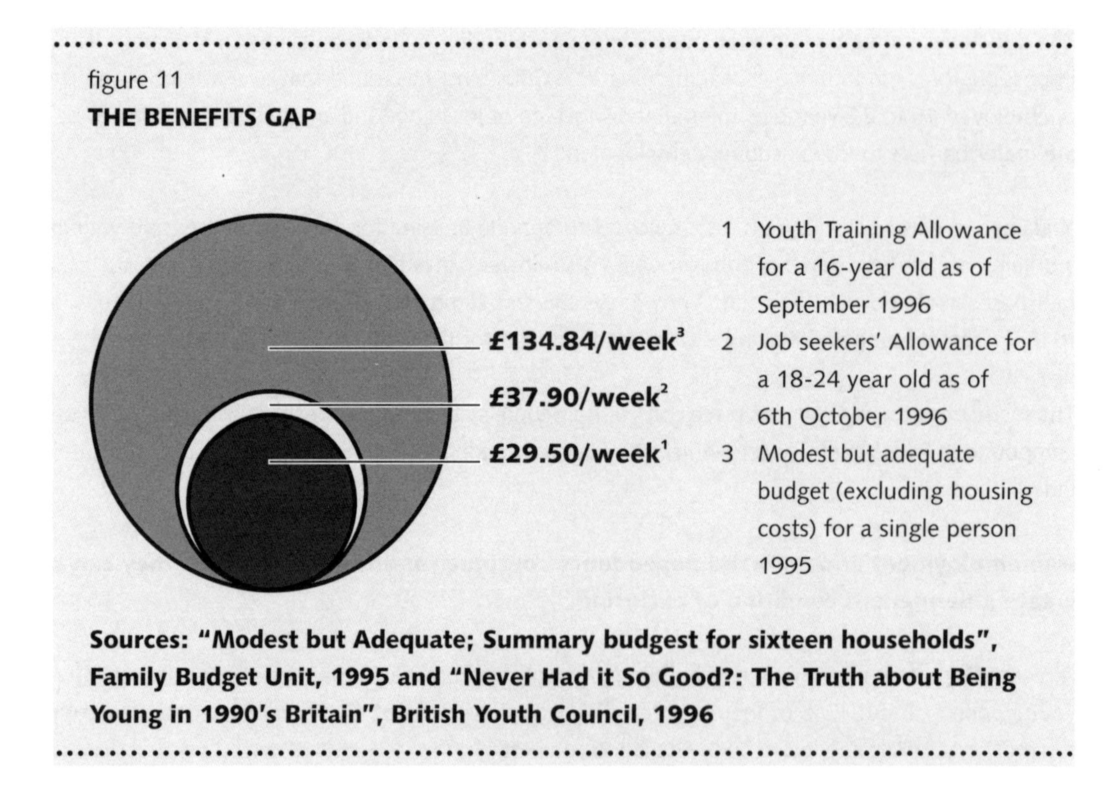

Sources: "Modest but Adequate; Summary budgest for sixteen households", Family Budget Unit, 1995 and "Never Had it So Good?: The Truth about Being Young in 1990's Britain", British Youth Council, 1996

The benefit system is clearly failing very many 16/17-year olds. The Government's promise of a YT place for all 16/17-year olds does not appear to have been fulfilled and the safety net of severe hardship payments, originally designed as a stop gap measure for a small number of cases, is unable to take the strain.

The number of 16/17-year olds claiming severe hardship payments has risen enormously since their introduction in September 1988. In March 1996, 10,323 awards were made compared with just 1,669 awards in May 1990. The success rate of applications has also risen, from just over 60% in 1988 to 78% in March 1996.[18] Despite a sixfold increase in awards, a number of agencies have expressed concern that many 16/17-year olds without a YT place do not receive hardship payments, although large numbers of them are in need.[19]

Of those 16/17-year olds who applied for severe hardship payments during September 1990:

- A tenth had been in care;
- A fifth had been physically or sexually abused;
- A third were homeless;
- Almost a half had no money at all.[20]

Benefits to 18 to 24-year olds were also reduced in 1988 and they are now treated as non-householders for benefit purposes unless they have children of their own. **18 to 24-year olds now have to manage on 79% of the allowance given to those who are 25 years or older.**

The Jobseeker's Allowance replaces Unemployment Benefit and Income Support for unemployed people from 7 Ocober 1996. Although a single allowance, there will still be a contribution-based and means-tested element. For the great majority of claimants, the introduction of the allowance will make no difference to the amount of benefit they receive each week.

The rates for young people eligible for contribution-based benefit (previously unemployment benefit) have, however, been reduced so that they are in line with the lower rates of Income Support paid to young people.

The contribution-based Job Seekers Allowance has been set at just £28.85 a week for those less than 18 years of age and £37.90 for 18 to 24 year olds, compared with £47.90 a week for those over 25 years of age. These changes mean that **a young person claiming contribution-based benefit after 7th October 1996 will receive around £10 less a week.**[21]

The emphasis of the new system is on getting unemployed people back to work. Claimants will be required to agree and follow a Jobseeker's Agreement which will outline the action a claimant must take to find work. If a claimant does not comply with the agreement strict sanctions can be applied including the withdrawal of benefit.

Many agencies have expressed concern that because of their disrupted lifestyles and other problems young homeless people could find it difficult adhering to a Jobseekers Agreement, particularly if it is insufficiently sensitive to their circumstances and is rigidly applied.[22]

In addition, changes to the Housing Benefit Eligibility Rules for under 25s have meant that there is often a gap between the local reference rent (LRR), which is set by local authorities as the maximum rent for Housing Benefit purposes, and what a landlord is charging.

The gap between Housing Benefit and rent levels will widen further from October 1996 when the LRR for single people under the age of 25 will be based upon shared not self-contained accommodation. These changes are intended to ensure that if young people do leave home they occupy 'modest accommodation' and aim to 'choose cheaper accommodation or to negotiate a lower rent with their landlords'.[23] And to ensure that young people on Housing Benefit do not take up accommodation which would lock them into dependence on benefits and prevent them from taking up modestly paid employment.[24]

There are, however, two fundamental flaws in the Government's rationale. Firstly, the rents charged by landlords are already often above the levels covered by Housing Benefit and the strong demand for rented properties means that landlords have no need to reduce rents - see A Shortage of Suitable Accommodation, page 39. Secondly, recent research, commissioned by the Department of the Environment, strongly suggests that Housing Benefit was never the passport to independence that the Government imagines.

Only a fifth of young people between the ages of 20 and 29 years who were living in the private rented sector in 1994/95 were in receipt of Housing Benefit (compared with around 60% of 20 to 29-year olds in the public sector). Also, many young private sector tenants who were eligible for benefit were not claiming it. The study concludes that *'benefit being available to young men and women able to find accommodation to rent clearly contributed little to the number living independently rather than with parents.'*[25]

Other benefit changes have also made it difficult for young people to secure independent accommodation. Even if a young person is able to afford regular rent, they often cannot afford the deposit and rent-in-advance payments that private landlords require before a tenancy commences.

If accommodation is unfurnished there is also the expense of equipping and furnishing the new home. Until 1988, anyone in receipt of Income Support could apply for a single payment to cover these one-off expenses. These grants have, however, been replaced by loans from the Social Fund which are discretionary and cash limited.

Furthermore, young people are not considered a priority for Social Fund loans and only in very limited circumstances are their applications successful.[26]

If a young person overcomes the considerable hurdles of finding and affording accommodation, research has shown that the chances of them settling and remaining in their new home will be significantly reduced if they cannot adequately furnish it.[26]

The rationale for these benefit reductions is that anyone who is young and single should be living in the parental home unless they can afford to cover the costs of living independently. However, many young people have no choice but to leave home and the costs of living independently are just the same for them as they are for the rest of the population.

Housing, food, fuel and council tax bills are not discounted to compensate for lower benefit payments. Indeed, it could be argued that the cost of living for young people who have left home is higher than average because of the substantial expenses of setting up home for the first time.

The Social Security Advisory Committee has challenged the justification for the changes and has strongly urged that *'at least for those living away from home, the full rate is restored'.* [27]

figure 12

THE STRAIN OF LOW BENEFIT LEVELS

Current benefit levels do not provide sufficient money for young people to live in independent accommodation. Housing and living costs mitigate against the sustaining of tenancies and attention needs to be focussed on the actual level of disposable income for young people moving to independence.

Strathclyde Regional Council

The withdrawal of benefits to most 16/17-year olds has caused great hardship.

The Home and Away Project, Lambeth

Poverty is a major problem for young people and the benefits system seems designed to prevent them getting the little money they are entitled to.

Stonham Housing Association

The limited availability of Income Support to young people is a contributory factor to the loss of, or inability to retain, accommodation.

Scottish Association of Citizens Advice Bureaux

Our experience indicates difficulties related to the ending of Income Support for 16/17-year olds and strong support amongst professional agencies for its reinstatement.

The Community Development Foundation

A major barrier is the problems young people encounter when they do eventually get accommodation - e.g. being unable to afford furniture. These issues can put an immense strain on the ability of young people to hold on to their accommodation.

The City Centre Initiative, Glasgow

LOW PAY

Employment does not always solve a young person's housing problems. Most young employed people are on low wages. **In 1995 weekly earnings for young people were as little as a third of the average** (Figure 13) and the gap between the amount earned by young people and others workers has grown by about a tenth over the past 10 years.[28]

With average weekly earnings of between £113 and £257 (depending on age and gender), young people who are in employment are clearly better off than their unemployed counterparts, but many still find they cannot afford to live independently. Private housing options, which are usually the only ones open to young people, are prohibitively expensive.

In addition, young people are much more likely to be in temporary or insecure forms of employment - the proportion of 16 to 24-year olds in temporary jobs is more than four times as high as for 24 to 55-year olds.[29]

Understandably, therefore, many young workers are cautious about making the considerable financial commitment of renting or buying their own home. Those who do buy property run a higher than average risk of losing it because of payment difficulties.[30]

figure 13
YOUNG PEOPLE'S EARNINGS, 1995

Under 18 Year Olds
Average weekly earnings were £113.40 for men and £117.10 for women.
Men earned 31% of average male earnings, and women 44% of average female earnings.

18 to 20 Year Olds
Average weekly earnings were £176.90 for men and £154.20 for women.
Men earned 48% of average male earnings and women 58% of average female earnings.

21 to 24 Year Olds
Average weekly earnings were £256.80 for men and £210.30 for women.
Men earned 69% of average male earnings and women 79% of average female earnings.

Source: New Earnings Survey, HMSO, 1995.

A SHORTAGE OF SUITABLE ACCOMMODATION

THE PRIVATE RENTED SECTOR

In most circumstances, young people are ineligible for public housing and have to look to the private sector for accommodation. The private rented sector has traditionally catered for young single people and in 1994/95 over a half (56%) of 20 to 24 year olds, who were living alone, were living in this type of accommodation.[31]

Many young people, however, experience considerable difficulties securing privately rented accommodation. Rent increases have exceeded the rate of inflation over recent years and rents are significantly higher than rents in the public sector.

For example, in 1994/95 the average weekly rent for a privately rented property was £70 compared with £37 for council homes and £46 for housing association properties.[32]

These differentials apply regardless of property type or region. Rents at this high level absorb a substantial proportion of a young person's modest earnings, leaving very little for other daily essentials. Young people on benefit, as demonstrated, experience even more difficulty affording privately rented accommodation.

Young people on low incomes also have to compete with their more affluent counterparts. There is growing evidence to suggest that young people who can afford home ownership are delaying buying and turning to the private rented sector instead.

A Department of the Environment study found that from 1991 to 1994/95 *'there was steep fall in owner-occupation among households in the 20 to 24 age range'* and an increase in the proportion that were tenants renting from private landlords.[31]

Other surveys, such as the Building Societies Mortgage Survey and Survey of Mortgage Lending, confirm this pattern. Although young people are still committed to home ownership in the long-term, their short-term confidence has been shaken by the housing market recession and the relatively high incidence of mortgage arrears, repossessions and negative equity, especially amongst young home-owners.[33]

Young people on benefit face additional access hurdles. According to recent research, many private landlords are reluctant to let homes or rooms to benefit claimants because of their 'undesirable image' and the delays they experience with Housing Benefit payments.

Three quarters of landlords say they would prefer to rent to someone who was working.[34] Some groups of young people, such as those from ethnic minorities and lesbians and gay men, are likely to find it even more difficult to secure and retain privately rented accommodation because of discriminatory attitudes and practices.

The private rented sector is still an important source of housing for young people. It is unencumbered by bureaucratic rules and processes and can provide readily accessible accommodation. However, high market rents and the substantial one-off payments required mean that many young people are excluded. Those who do rent privately are often concentrated in the poorest quality stock, with few facilities and little security. Although such accommodation may be acceptable or tolerable in the short-term, it rarely constitutes a secure, long-term home.

Bed and breakfast hotels are particularly unsuitable for vulnerable young people. Many reports have catalogued the poor and unsafe conditions to be found in this type of accommodation.[35] Over recent years local authorities have reduced their use of bed and breakfast hotels as temporary accommodation for homeless families in recognition of their inappropriateness.[36] However, recent research indicates that many single people are now using hotels, either making their own booking or being directed to them by voluntary agencies.[37]

Many of these single people have mental health or drug/alcohol dependency problems, and harrassment of residents by landlords and other residents is relatively common-place. The combination of poor physical conditions and the ever-present risk of intimidation and violence means that, in most cases, bed and breakfast hotels cannot be considered suitable accommodation for young people.

figure 14
ACCOMODATION FOR YOUNG PEOPLE IN THE PRIVATE SECTOR

There are more young single people in housing need than any other group but they experience most difficulty finding private rented accommodation and as a result, competition for tenancies is extreme. As an illustration, at 31st July 1995, there were 12 single homeless people with council approval for a tenancy deposit, yet they have been unable to find any form of tenancy despite the assistance of Housing Advice.
Stevenage Borough Council

The deposit and rent in advance required for private accommodation normally totals more than £1,000, meaning that without some form of grant, such accommodation is beyond the means of most young people.
Home and Away Project, Lambeth

The shortage of affordable housing in the private sector, which young people have traditionally used as a first step to independence, has also fuelled the increase in youth homelessness.
National Federation of Housing Associations

Many young people who live in rented accommodation can only afford sub-standard accommodation in the most run-down areas.
Community Development Foundation

HOME OWNERSHIP

Given the weak economic position of most young people, home ownership is a realistic option for only a very small minority. In 1995, the average price paid by first-time buyers was £45,341 and the average advance £40,655. On average, therefore, first-time buyers required about £5,000 as a deposit and an annual income of some £14,000 to support a mortgage (assuming an advance/income ratio of 3).

It is clear that with high unemployment, low wages and an increasingly insecure employment market, relatively few young people are in a position to afford to become home-owners.

PUBLIC HOUSING

Council housing primarily caters for families and access for young single people is generally limited to the emergency routes provided by homelessness and community care legislation and Children Act[39] (access via these emergency routes is discussed in more detail in *Failure of the Welfare Safety Nets*, page 43).

The underlying assumption is that young people without dependents are not vulnerable and can fend for themselves. This view is reflected in both the types of housing provided by the public sector and the access rules and priorities that public landlords apply.

About a quarter of council stock is one bedroom but a large proportion of this is designated for use by elderly people.[40] The shortage of small units clearly has a significant impact on the ability of local councils to assist young single people but there is reason to believe that the waiting list and allocations policies of many councils are, in addition, unnecessarily unfavourable.

A Chartered Institute of Housing survey of council allocations' policies in England and Wales in 1990 found that:[41]

- A fifth of councils did not include young single people on their waiting lists;
- A third (33%) of councils would not grant tenancies to young people under the age of 18;
- 81% of councils that did grant tenancies to under 18-year olds required a guarantor as evidence that the young person had family or agency support.

Historically, housing associations have played a complementary role to councils by providing smaller units and special schemes for people who would not usuually receive priority for council housing. In 1994/95, for example, a half of all housing association properties in Britain were bedsits or one bedroom flats.[40]

Despite their enhanced profile over recent years housing associations are still relatively minor stock holders - in 1994/95 they owned 17% of all public housing and 4% of the total housing stock[42] - they are therefore able to rehouse only a small proportion of homeless young people.

Furthermore, new housing association developments are more likely to be for families than single people. Local authority spending restrictions, an emphasis on councils as the enablers rather than direct providers of housing, and increased rates of statutory homelessness have placed pressures on associations to provide more family housing. In 1988, 65% of new housing association lets were of one bedroom accommodation compared with only 27% in 1994/95.[43]

Additionally, there is some evidence that councils and housing associations are increasingly reluctant to rehouse young single people because of the management problems they experience.

A number of voluntary agencies reported to the inquiry that they were finding it more difficult than ever to persuade councils and housing associations to let properties to young people.

This is a disturbing trend which threatens to further restrict the housing options of young people. It would be foolish to pretend that all young single people make model tenants and never create management problems. However, difficulties are most likely to arise if young people are rehoused in hard-to-let housing, away from their local area and with little or no support and supervision. In part 2 we discuss the importance to young people of sensitive allocations and continued support following rehousing.

figure 15
GRANTING TENANCIES TO 16/17-YEAR OLDS

There has been some confusion over the legality of granting tenancies to 16/17-year olds which has sometimes caused difficulties in housing them.
National Federation of Housing Associations

For 16/17-year olds it is especially difficult to access 2nd stage accommodation as many organisations remain unwilling to offer tenancies. Very few social service departments will underwrite licenses or tenancies. This makes it harder for this group to access the private rented sector as well as other options.
Arlington Housing Association

Only a very small minority of young single people are, therefore, likely to gain access to mainstream public housing, although their need is clearly growing. A Department of the Environment study of council waiting lists in 1986 and 1991 found that *'the most striking change from 1986 was the large increase in the proportion of younger applicants'.*

In 1991, 43% of applicants who had been on a waiting list for less than six months (the indicator used for new applicants) were under 25 years of age.[44] This is a remarkably high proportion given that 16 to 24-year olds represent just 17% of the adult population.

FAILURE OF THE WELFARE SAFETY NETS

There are a number of Government provided safety nets that should catch and support young people who are homeless and vulnerable. There is the Children Act 1989, homelessness legislation[39] and community care legislation (the NHS and Community Care Act 1990).

These laws place duties on local authorities to provide housing and support to young people who are homeless or in danger of becoming homeless. There is strong evidence, however, that these safety nets are failing large numbers of young people in need.

CHILDREN ACT 1989

Although the Children Act has certainly improved the overall situation for young homeless people,[45] there is evidence that many local authorities do not rank youth homelessness as a priority issue.

A survey of councils in England and Wales, undertaken by CHAR in 1993[45] found that:

- Only three quarters of councils had a policy of assessing all homeless 16/17-years olds who approach them to establish whether they were entitled to accommodation under the Children Act;
- Only just over a half (59%) of councils usually considered a 16/17-year old living on the streets to be 'in need' under the terms of the legislation, in spite of the obvious risks that a young person in this situation faces;
- The great majority of councils had not undertaken an assessment of the needs of homeless 16/17-year olds in their area;
- Around a third of social service departments had not developed joint policies with housing departments.

The study concludes that *'social service departments are, in the main, failing to fulfil their responsibilities to homeless 16/17-year olds under the Children Act.'* A survey of Welsh social service authorities by Shelter Cymru found a similarly disappointing record in Wales.[46]

figure 16

SOCIAL SERVICES DEPARTMENTS' RESPONSIBILITIES TO HOMELESS 16/17 YEAR OLDS UNDER THE CHILDREN ACT 1989

Local authorities have to provide accommodation for any child in need in their area, who has reached the age of 16, if their welfare would be seriously prejudiced without such accommodation (Section 20(3)).

Broader duties are included in Section 17 which states that a local authority has a duty to safeguard and promote the welfare of children in their area who are in need and to promote the upbringing of such children by their families, by providing a range and level of services appropriate to these children's needs .

Section 17 duties are more extensive and enduring since they lead to *'advice, assistance and befriending until the young person is 21'*, regular statutory reviews and the young person being brought within the care system. Section 24 includes local authority duties to young people leaving care.

HOMELESSNESS LEGISLATION

Homelessness legislation, which was introduced in England and Wales in 1985, Scotland in 1987 and extended to Northern Ireland in 1988,[39] places a duty on local authorities to provide those who are unintentionally homeless and in priority need with permanent accommodation.

Single people are usually only accepted for rehousing under the legislation if they are defined as vulnerable for some reason and so in priority need. However, the Code of Guidance accompanying the legislation stresses that age alone should not confer vulnerability (unless it is old age),[47] and so **few authorities automatically define young homeless people as vulnerable, even if they are only 16 or 17 years of age and are sleeping rough. Only if a young person has a problem in addition to their homelessness will they be considered as potentially eligible, but even then there is a strong possibility that they will not be accepted for housing.**

A survey of local authorities in England and Wales, undertaken by CHAR in 1993,[48] found that:

- Only a half of authorities would usually define as vulnerable an applicant who is a young person who has left care;
- Only two-fifths of authorities would usually define a young person with drug and/or alcohol dependency problems as vulnerable;
- Only a quarter of authorities would usually define a young person who is sleeping rough as vulnerable.

Many young people do not get as far as being formally assessed under homelessness legislation. In 1993 less than three-quarters (71%) of councils in England and Wales had a policy of assessing all homeless 16/17-year olds who approached them.[47]

It appears likely that legislation on homelessness, in the shape of the New Housing Bill, will continue to fail young homeless people and the possibility of them securing decent long-term accommodation will be further diminished.

The Housing Bill 1996 proposes that the duty on local authorities in England and Wales to provide permanent accommodation to eligible homeless households should be replaced with an obligation to provide only temporary accommodation for a period of up to 24 months.
If enacted, this would mean that young people who do qualify under the legislation are likely to face a series of short-term private sector lets rather than a period of stability in long-term accommodation.

COMMUNITY CARE

The primary aim of care in the community is to develop community-based alternatives to residential care. Social service departments have the lead responsibility for conducting assessments of care needs and providing appropriate care packages.

However, the emphasis on personal rather than housing needs, and on specific priority groups (such as people with mental health problems, frail elderly people, people with drug or alcohol related problems) has meant that young homeless people are often overlooked. A number of studies have found that social services departments will only generally find a young homeless person eligible under the community care legislation if they have a problem or a reason for vulnerability that is additional to their age.[49]

In addition, **social services departments and the community care planning process tend to be organised by client group, and so young people with multiple problems often miss the net entirely.**

While all local authorities produce a separate plan for children under the Children Act, most of the community care plans surveyed for this report did not address the care and accommodation needs of young care leavers moving into adulthood, or alternative strategies for young homeless people not provided with accommodation.
Right to Care:Good practice in community care planning for single homeless people, CHAR, 1993.

Although there are three different legislative safety nets which should individually or jointly protect young homeless people, it appears that many young people are still going without the help, support and protection they need.

A young person is most likely to be helped if he/she falls into one of the more traditional need categories - for example, if they have a mental health problem, a physical disability or a learning difficulty.

However, one of the problems is that many authorities reject young single applicants without a full assessment interview, and so additional needs often do not come to light. Also, because mental health and psychological disorders are usually associated with older single homeless people, officers are not always alert to the possibility that young people may have similar problems.

There are a number of reasons why existing legislation is failing to help young people who are so clearly in need. Limited resources have to be targeted and young people are rarely deemed a priority compared with other groups in need.
There is also a critical shortage of appropriate accommodation and support services. In addition, some statutory definitions and responsibilities overlap allowing authorities to more easily evade and transfer responsibility, especially in respect of the more complex and needy cases.

Agencies tend to define young people's needs according to their own profesional boundaries and this means that some of the more complex and multi-faceted cases are seen either as on the margin or outside of any one agency's responsibility. Co-ordination between different departments and agencies is also often poor. **The consequence of these failures is that a growing number of very vulnerable young homeless people are living in precarious and often dangerous situations, on the streets and in run down squats and bed and breakfast hotels.**

figure 17

LEGISLATION - FAILING TO MEET THE NEEDS OF HOMELESS YOUNG PEOPLE

Young people's housing needs have been exacerbated by the failure of the major pieces of legislation affecting them - the Children Act, the NHS and Community Care Act and the Housing Act 1985 - to work together. Differences in definition and responsibility have meant that young people fall between the gaps.
National Federation of Housing Associations

Whilst some housing authorities will house young people, there is generally a reluctance and often internal disputes with social services departments regarding overlapping responsibilities under the Children Act and homelessness legislation.
Barnardos

The needs of a drifting population are not best met by a system which is based on local connection, services which might prevent a deterioration in mental health are conspicuous by their absence, and the bureaucracy in local authorities which can lead to a 16-year old with mental health and drug problems being passed between three different areas of social services.
The London Connection Day Centre

PART 1

No choice but to leave

Research has shown that in areas and times of economic hardship, the proportion of young people living with their parents rises. For example, the National Child Development Study has found that in areas of high unemployment, *'men's departures into partnerships and women's chances of living with friends or others are significantly reduced.'* [1]

Many young people find they are unable to establish a home of their own and have no option but to remain within the parental home for longer than they (and often their parents) would wish.

A survey undertaken for the Department of the Environment in 1995 found that the number of young people between the ages of 20 and 24 years living at home had increased significantly since 1991, with over a half of all men and a third of women were still living with their parents.[2] A recent survey of family lifestyles by Mintel also found that over half of young people between the ages of 20 and 24 years were still living with their parents, as were a fifth of 25 to 34 year olds.[3] This finding contradicts the common perception that young people today are less likely to live at home than in previous generations.

figure 18

LEAVING HOME PUT IN CONTEXT

It is frequently assumed that young people are independent at a much younger age than earlier generations. Indeed, much current Government policy is intended to stem this seemingly hedonistic flow. However, this view is based on a misinterpretation of the reality faced by young people and of young people's aspirations. The great majority of 16 to 24-years olds live with their parents and most do not expect to leave home until they are *at least* 18 years of age.[4]

There is little doubt that if they had the choice many young people who live with their parents would prefer to live independently. However, unemployment, low wages and benefit rates and high housing costs have meant that it is probably more difficult now than at any other time for young people to make the transition to independence. The shortage of employment and housing opportunities has meant that the transition to independence has become more difficult, fractured and prolonged, and many more young people now return home at least once before finally leaving home.[5]

This is in sharp contrast to the leaving home experience of their parents' generation. In the 1950s and 1960s it was common for young people to leave home, marry and start families within a relatively short period of time. Indeed, leaving home and marriage were so closely entwined that in social surveys the age of marriage was often taken as a proxy for the age of leaving home.[6] Although this pattern is often considered the normal one, it has had a relatively short life.

Before the Second World War, the transition out of the parental home started at a young age and was frequently protracted, often including a number of stages between the parental home and the marital one. Young people frequently lodged with other families or lived in apprenticeship hostels, until they had the resources to set up an independent home.[7]

It is likely that many young people today would also appreciate the opportunity to have a period of independence between leaving the parental home and getting married or living with a partner. However, with the exception of going away to college or university, there are currently few means of them achieving this.

We are not suggesting that there ever was a 'golden age' when the process of leaving home and becoming independent was typically smooth and untroubled. The journey from childhood to adulthood has always been difficult as young people make their journey to independence.

What has changed, however, is that the relatively secure pathways that young people have traditionally taken have become less sure, with the consequence that many more young people are becoming homeless.

It is not possible for all young people to remain within the parental home until they have the opportunity or resources to make a safe journey to independence. A range of pressures, such as changing family structures and relationships, financial pressures and poor housing conditions, have increased tensions at home sometimes to the point where a young person has no option but to leave.

When young people leave home because of family conflict they are much more likely to do so in an unplanned way with few resources and no family support. Faced with only very limited housing options they are highly vulnerable to homelessness.

It is at this point that welfare services should intervene to help young people and to prevent homelessness. However, as demonstrated in Section 2, very many young homeless people fall outside or through the welfare safety nets that are meant to catch and safeguard them.

UNABLE TO REMAIN AT HOME

The difficulties experienced by many young people force them to remain dependent on their families at an age when they might have expected to become independent.

As long as relations with parents are good, or at least tolerable, this arrangement is acceptable until a young person has the resources and opportunity to be able to set up their own home. For a growing minority of young people, however, remaining within the parental home is not an option.

Many are forced to leave home because of family conflict or tensions, whilst those in local authority care have no option but to make their own way once they reach the age of 18, although many leave much earlier.

FAMILY CONFLICT - A KEY FACTOR

There is no doubt that family conflict is the most important immediate or trigger cause of homelessness amongst young people. In local survey findings submitted to the inquiry, family problems accounted for between one and two thirds of those in housing need with a median of around 40%. Other surveys have put the proportion even higher.[7]

This emphasis on family friction is understandable since information on the reasons for homelessness is usually collected directly from young people themselves and the most recent and tangible problem is bound to be upper-most in their minds. However, the causes of homelessness are more diverse and run deeper than the catch-all phrase 'family conflict' suggests.

This is not to down-grade the significance of family conflict - it is how young people themselves see their situation and there is no doubt that family breakdown can cause immense stress and hardship. An appreciation of the role played by family relations is important if initiatives aimed at preventing homelessness are to be effective.

figure 19

FAMILY CONFLICT AND YOUTH HOMELESSNESS

Young people who leave home because of family friction are much more likely to become homeless than those who leave for other reasons - 20% compared with 2%. The younger a person is when they leave home the more likely they are to become homeless - 25% of 16/17-year olds who leave home because of family friction become homeless compared with 19% of 18/19-year olds.

Leaving Home, G. Jones, 1995.

The single largest cause of youth homelessness is the breakdown of family relationships.
The Hackney Youth Unemployment Project

A significant number of young people become homeless as a result of family breakdown. This may be the result of the breakdown of a relationship and/or divorce. It may be the result of overcrowding and/or the pressures created by poor housing and unemployment.
The London Connection, day centre.

Young people very rarely leave home on a whim. They leave for specific reasons which are often the culmination of years of a severe problem.
St Basils, Birmingham

90% of our clients just cannot return to their family home. They have sad histories of physical, sexual and mental abuse, family split-ups and poverty.
HYPED Project, Eastern Dorset

ARE YOUNG PEOPLE PUSHED OR DO THEY JUMP?

A common perception is that, disgruntled with the tensions and compromises of family life and lured by the promises of independence, young people jump irresponsibly into homelessness. However, evidence shows that this is not the experience of the majority of young homeless people.

Most have not left home on a whim or impulse, but have been pushed into leaving because of long standing and serious conflict with their families. For example, research recently undertaken by Centrepoint, with 7,500 homeless young people in seven different locations across the country, found that 86% had been forced to leave home rather than choosing to leave.[8]

This is in marked contrast to a survey conducted by Centrepoint in 1987, which found that pull factors such as moving to find work or needing to be independent were far more prominent and were mentioned by a half of all young homeless people compared to just 14% in 1996.

Indeed, research suggests that in a significant minority of cases, 'family conflict' masks much more serious problems such as physical or sexual abuse.- see figure 20:

figure 20
YOUTH HOMELESSNESS AND ABUSE AT HOME

40% of young women who become homeless have experienced sexual abuse in childhood or adolescence.[10]

Family breakdown through physical or sexual abuse is a common cause of young people coming to Patrick House. Although this is a well documented cause of teenage homelessness, I feel it is important to make the point that dysfunctioning parents can and often do lead to youngsters becoming homeless.
The Society of St Dismas

There is a strong connection between running away and abuse in the home.
The Children's Society

Contrary to popular belief, young people do not run away in search of bright lights, they are more likely to be running from troubles and problems at home, wanting to escape what has become an intolerable situation. For many, the streets are safer than where they were living.
Childline Cymru

The true extent of abuse that has been experienced by young homeless people is likely to be higher since many young people will be reluctant to reveal the truth. For example, the Scottish Association of Citizens Advice Bureaux says that *'the problems of abuse and violence are often not reported initially and are disguised amongst the figures given for household friction or parental problems.'*[11]

Young people made homeless because of abuse or neglect within the family will be very vulnerable. Most will have left home early, will be unsupported by their parents, emotionally traumatised and are more likely than other young homeless people to end up sleeping rough, with all the dangers and difficulties that entails.

The fact that family conflict is often serious is supported by several different surveys which have found that the majority of young homeless people say they are unable to return home.[12]

FAMILIES UNDER PRESSURE

The high incidence of family conflict is not surprising given the pressures that many families experience. At the same time that young people are expected to remain dependent on their families for longer, changes to family structures and relationships and growing economic pressures make family relations more fraught.

Many families experience difficulties and tensions because of their low incomes, and evidence strongly suggests that the number of families who experience poverty has increased significantly over recent years.

figure 21

CHANGING PATTERNS OF POVERTY

- While average income in the UK rose by 37% between 1979 and 1992/93, the poorest section of the population saw their income fall by 18%.[13]
- By 1992, almost a quarter (24%) of the population (13.7 million) was on or below the level of income support compared with just over a tenth (11%) in 1979.[14]
- One in every three children is now growing up in poverty compared with one in ten in 1979.[15]
- Increasing numbers of households have no earners, up from 5% in 1979 to 20% in 1994/5.[16]

Poverty is not just about being unable to afford to buy and do the things that other households take for granted - it is about stress and anxiety, health problems, poor housing, overcrowding, family breakdown and impoverished 'life-chances'. The children of poor families are more likely to have poor health, to be poorly educated and trained and to end up unemployed and homeless.[17]

To compound problems, families on benefit often lose income when a dependent child becomes a 'non-dependent' adult. The welfare benefit system penalises them twice - their Housing Benefit and Income Support are reduced and they lose Child Benefit since it is assumed that they are no longer financially responsible for the young person.

This is starkly contradicted by the cuts to benefits for under 25 year olds, introduced on the grounds that young people should be at least partly dependent on their parents. The National Housing Forum has calculated that, at worst, these benefit cuts can reduce the parents' income by half.[18]

When money is tight it is not surprising that prolonged dependency leads to escalating tensions between a young person and their parents. In the majority of cases such tensions are contained and do not lead to homelessness; young people with poor economic prospects and whose families are on low incomes tend to leave home later than their more affluent counterparts.[19] However, in a growing number of cases these tensions and difficulties act as the trigger to homelessness.

figure 22

YOUTH HOMELESSNESS AND FAMILIES UNDER PRESSURE

We have had several parents tell (us) that they are evicting their children because they cannot afford to look after them at home. This trend appears to contradict the Government's position on supporting the family.

The Home and Away Project, Lambeth

Young homeless people often come from families who are living in poor accommodation... and... tensions increase as children grow up.
YMCA

In this area a large proportion of people with low incomes live in flatted estates - a type of accommodation that is found to be increasingly inflexible in meeting the needs of growing families. The success of this type of accommodation in meeting changing needs relied on a system of easy transfers, a system which has been eroded over the past 15 years. The resulting pressure on families in flats which are too small plays a part in aggravating family difficulties.
Consortium (South East London)

Overcrowding and poor housing conditions are also often contributory factors. Although the housing situation for the great majority has greatly improved over recent years, a significant minority of households have experienced a marked decline in their living conditions. In 1991 around 200,000 households were sharing their accommodation with another family - an increase of 17% on 1981.[20]

Around 285,000 children now live in accommodation shared with other families and the chance of any particular child living like this has increased by about 10% over the past decade. However, it is households who are disadvantaged more generally, such as one parent families and black and other ethnic minority families, who have seen the most significant deterioration in their housing situation.

For example, over the past ten years the children of one-parent families have experienced a 74% increase in the likelihood of their living in temporary accommodation, whereas the chances of this happening to the children of other households has fallen by 18%.

Changes to family structure, through the separation and divorce of parents and the creation of new partnerships, have definitely played a part in increasing the pressures experienced by families.

There is evidence that the children of lone parents and parents who have formed new partnerships are more likely to leave home at an early age and to become homeless.

A survey of young Scottish people[21] found that:

- 44% of those with a step parent left home by the age of 19 compared with 33% of those with lone parents and 27% of those with both parents;
- A quarter of homeless young people had a step parent compared with 4% of all young Scottish people.

Other studies have found a similar pattern.[22] It is important to note, however, that this correlation could be due to other factors shared by these households such as low incomes and poor housing conditions. Recent research also suggests that it is the quality of family relations that matter not family structure.

One study has found that the amount of time young people spend with their families and the ways in which families communicate and resolve conflict are more influential on the development of children and young people than the type of family.[23]

Quality family life provides a feeling of security; it educates them in the skills that enable a person to live independently. In addition, it acts as a support network that remains accessible to a young person, very often throughout and beyond their youth. Many young people, however, have not experienced quality family life - they are told they are not wanted and the network of support, practical, social, financial and emotional, is not available.
St Anne's, Leeds

Given the considerable pressures that many families experience, it is perhaps not surprising that so many of these situations result in family conflict and tension and young people becoming homeless. However, it is not only young people with disadvantaged backgrounds who become homeless. Many agencies involved with young people have reported to the inquiry that they are seeing growing numbers of young people from comfortable middle class backgrounds who are estranged from, and unsupported by, their parents.

LEAVING HOME WITHOUT SUPPORT

Setting up home for the first time is an expensive business and very few young people are in a position to be self-financing. Most benefit from substantial amounts of financial and practical support during the transition to independence - in the form of educational grants, college-or university-provided accommodation and money and gifts from parents and other family members.

Emotional support and the opportunity to return to the protective environment of home for short periods, or if things go wrong, are crucial elements in the transition to independence.

A college or university education for example allows a young person to experiment with independence. Halls of residence provide an environment that is less restrictive than home or school but where a young person does not have to take on the full responsibilities of running their own home, and college life provides social and support networks that young people need to help them shape their own identities.

Research suggests that young people who do not receive support when they leave home are significantly less likely to make a successful transition to independence and are, therefore, more likely to experience poverty and homelessness.[24]

A study of young homeless Scottish people found that nine out of 11 who had received little or no support from their families when they left home subsequently became homeless.[24] The study concluded that *'family support is an important element in the successful establishment of an independent home, and structural problems including the inadequacy of young people's incomes and the lack of affordable housing for young people leaving home, are exacerbated when family support is not forthcoming.'*

figure 23
RITES OF PASSAGE: CONTRASTING TRANSITIONS TO INDEPENDENCE

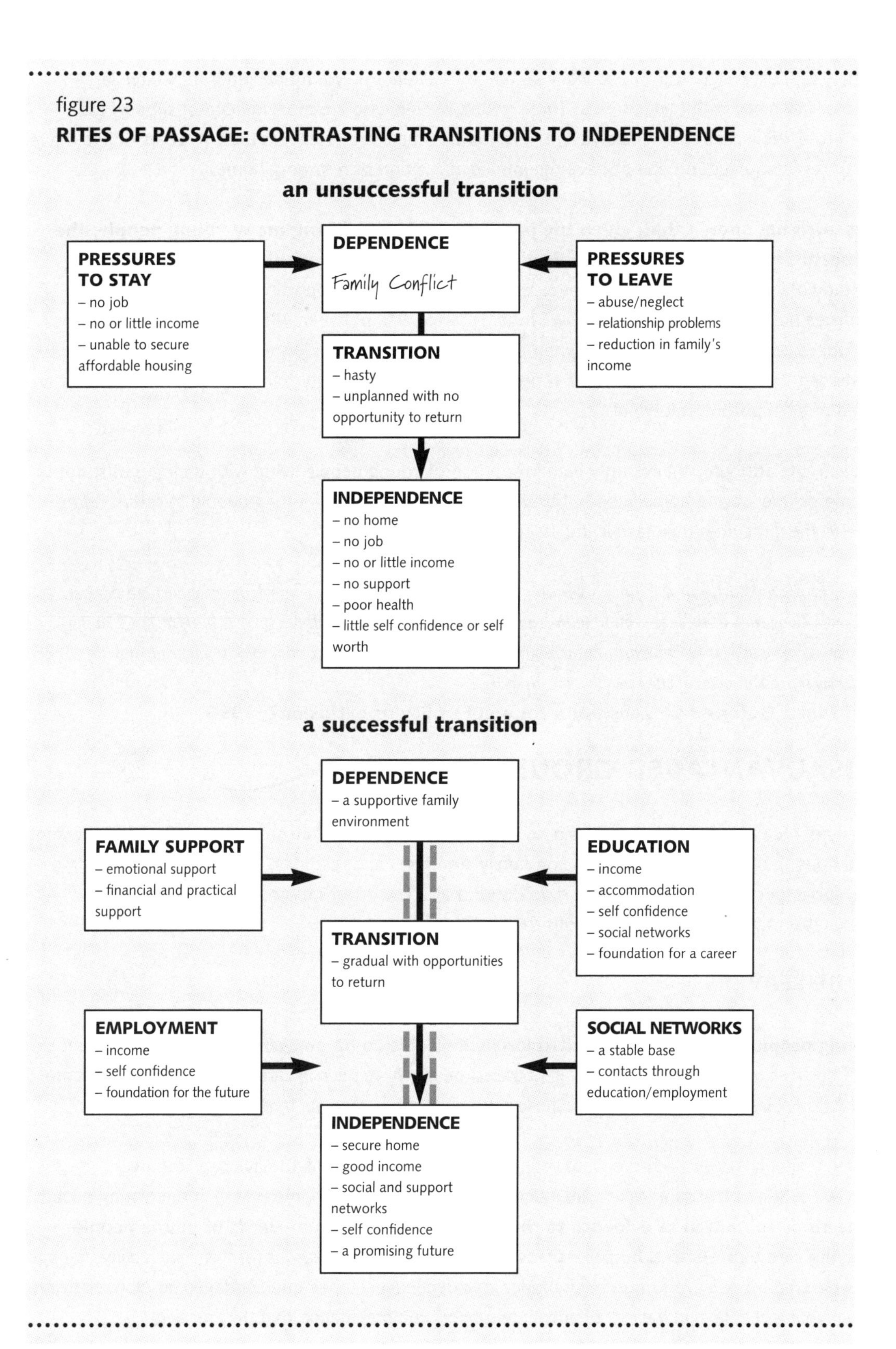

Family support is significantly less likely be made available to a young person if they have left care or fallen out with their parents. Those young people who are most in need of support are, therefore, the least likely to receive it. These young people are often less than 18 years of age, have no or few resources and do not have the immediate option of returning home.

Research has shown that, given the harsh environment facing many young people, the opportunity to return home is critically important to the prevention of homelessness. A study of young Scottish people, for example, found that the proportion of home-leavers who returned home to live by age 19 *doubled* from 15% to 29% between 1987 and 1991. The author, Gill Jones, concludes that at a time when the pathways to independence have become more extended, complex and fractured for young people, the opportunity to return home has become an even more important safety net.

Indeed, she attributes the recently high proportion of young people living with their parents, not to young people leaving home later, but to the increased tendency of young people to return home due to the difficulties they face living independently.

Young people are having to reorganise their lives in different ways to capitalise on whatever opportunities exist. Progress along each of these transition paths can become less certain - sometimes there is backtracking. Young people may give up courses, or return to their parental homes, because they cannot afford independent living. The ordering of transition events has become less prescribed.
Gill Jones, Deferred Citizenship: a coherent policy of exclusion?, 1996

DISADVANTAGED GROUPS

Many of the causes of homelessness described above, such as low incomes, the lack of employment and housing opportunities and changing family structures and relations, affect young people across the social spectrum. However, there is no doubt that some groups of young people are more vulnerable than others to the situations that create homelessness.

CARE-LEAVERS

Young people leaving care are particularly vulnerable to homelessness. Surveys have found that between a fifth and a half of young homeless people have been in care, and that care-leavers are particularly over-represented amongst those sleeping rough or living in temporary accommodation.[25]

Given that only 1% of all children and young people under the age of 18 have been in care, this clearly shows that care-leavers are much more likely to become homeless than other young people. **One study submitted as evidence to the inquiry found that two-thirds of young people leaving care experienced homelessness.** There are three main reasons for this vulnerability: the age at which most care leavers make the transition to independence; their disadvantaged position relative to other young people; and the lack of adequate support and preparation that they receive.

Leaving care at a young age

Care-leavers are expected to make the transition to independence at a much younger age than other young people. Around two thirds have left care by their 18th birthday, whereas the average age of leaving home for other young people is around 22 years.[26]

Some young people are themselves eager to leave care as soon as they are able to, but there are indications that financial and workload pressures have created an incentive for social services departments to move young people on as quickly as possible. Significantly, **leaving care is almost always a once-only event with no opportunity to return should a young person experience difficulties.** Young people who have left the parental home, on the other hand, usually return home at least once before making the final break.[24]

A disadvantaged position

Young people who leave care are disadvantaged in a number of ways. They are often without family support and are more likely to have few or no qualifications and to be unemployed or on a low income. They may also have emotional or psychological problems because of experiences of family breakdown, abuse and/or living in care. Many experience frequent moves between care homes, foster parents and the parental home.[27]

About half the care-leavers seen by Centrepoint during 1994 did not have any qualifications,[9] while a Leeds University study of young people leaving care found the proportion to be even higher at 75%.[28] Having no or few qualifications means that care leavers are disadvantaged in the job market. Research shows that around half are unemployed, compared with 15% of young people generally.[29]

Low or no income is, consequently, a major problem for care leavers. The great majority are on benefits but training and benefit rates for under 25 year olds are based on the assumption that young people are living with their parents. This does not reflect the reality for young people who have left care. The great majority (80%) of care-leavers have been in the position of having no money at all.[30]

Inadequate preparation and support

Despite the multiple disadvantages they face care-leavers have no automatic right to housing. The main responsibility for helping young people leaving care lies with social services departments. Under the Children Act 1989 and its regulations and guidance, social services have duties and powers to provide accommodation and support to care-leavers.

Although the Children Act has had many positive effects on the preparation for independence and after-care services provided to young people (for example, by improving inter-agency cooperation), a shortage of resources and the discretionary status of many of the provisions mean that the quality of services is very inconsistent.

- In 1992, a half of local authorities did not have a policy statement or guidelines for care leavers' support.[31]
- About a half of young people leaving care do not receive a Leaving Care Grant.[31]
- A half of local authorities do not define young people leaving care as vulnerable under the homelessness legislation.[32]
- Around a quarter (23%) of young people who have left care say they had no support from any source.[31]

Given the disadvantages that many care-leavers experience and the frequent failures of the system to provide support when it is needed, it is not surprising that many find themselves homeless or in poor quality accommodation, with little or no money, few prospects and feelings of isolation, loneliness and depression.

YOUNG PEOPLE FROM BLACK AND OTHER ETHNIC MINORITIES

Black and other ethnic minority young people who are homeless are more likely to be living in hidden situations (for example, staying with family or friends) than sleeping rough and are less likely to approach advice agencies. Their problems are, therefore, more easily overlooked.

A study of young homeless people in three different regions undertaken in 1995 found that *'young Blacks and Asians were more likely to have stayed with friends and/or relatives. White homeless were most likely to turn to statutory and voluntary agencies for support, black homeless were less likely, and Asian homeless least likely of all.'*[33]

figure 24

HOMELESSNESS AMONGST BLACK AND OTHER ETHNIC MINORITIES

A CHAR and Federation of Black Housing Organisations' Conference on the Children Act and Young Black Homeless People held in 1994 concluded that because young black people were more likely to stay with friends or relatives, they were overlooked by *'housing policies that provide only short term solutions to young people who are on the streets.'*[34]

Federation of Black Housing Associations and CHAR, 1995.

A Department of the Environment survey found that a quarter of homeless applicants to nine English local authorities in 1992/93 were black (16%), Asian (4%) or from some other ethnic minority group (5%)[35], although in 1991 people from ethnic minorities represented just 5.5% of the national population.[36] In London the proportion of homeless applicants who were from ethnic minorities rose to over half (52%).[35]

Study of Homeless Applicants, Department of the Environment, 1996.

A Centrepoint survey of young people who approached homeless agencies in England and Northern Ireland during 1994/95 found that over two fifths of those who applied were from black or ethnic minority groups, while in London, the proportion was much higher at 54%.
The New Picture of Youth Homelessness in Britain, Centrepoint, 1996.[37]

Research undertaken in Croydon found that 37% of young homeless people within the Borough were black while in the 1991 Census this group accounted for only 8% of the local population.
Evidence submitted to the inquiry.

The high incidence of homelessness amongst black and ethnic minority young people is illustrated by the fact that, in spite of the greater likelihood of them living in 'hidden situations' and their greater reluctance to approach agencies for help, they are still over-represented amongst young people approaching homeless agencies.

Black and other ethnic minority young people are more vulnerable to homelessness because they are more likely to experience the problems that lead to homelessness. For example, they are more likely to be unemployed, on low incomes and living in poor housing conditions.

In 1994 the male unemployment rate for all minority ethnic groups stood at 25% compared with 11% for white men.[38] The differences are even more dramatic when one focuses just on young people. For example, 37% of economically active black Caribbean men aged between 16 and 24 were unemployed compared with 18% of their white counterparts.[38]

In deprived areas this proportion is even higher - indeed, in some areas it is not uncommon for the great majority of young black people to be out of work. Black people are also more likely to be living in substandard accommodation - according to 1991 Census data - for example, they are more likely to be overcrowded and to have to share bathroom and toilet facilities with other families.[20]

Young black people are also more likely to experience disadvantage and discrimination when they look for accommodation. High unemployment and low wages place young people in a weak market position, but there is also evidence to show that white people in the same position fare better when it comes to access to accommodation.

A number of studies have demonstrated how discrimination and racism operate in the private housing markets.[39] There is also evidence that black people are less likely to be rehoused through public housing channels.

A 1992/93 Department of the Environment study of homeless applicants, found that black people made up 16% of all those who applied but accounted for 12% of those accepted and 20% of those rejected under the homelessness legislation.[35]

YOUNG REFUGEES AND ASYLUM SEEKERS

In 1995, the Refugee Council accommodated 2,591 asylum seekers and refugees and almost a half (48%) of these were between 17 and 25 years of age.[40] Many, like Abdul whose story is described below, arrive in this country alone and with nowhere to go. The Refugee Council has considerable problems securing suitable accommodation for its clients. In most cases it has no option but to use private lettings and bed and breakfast hotels, although it says that the system is fraught with potential for abuse and exploitation and demand outstrips supply.

A common arrangement even for those we do place is for 2,3 or 4 people to be sharing a room, with total strangers who may not even have a common language. How many stay put we do not know. Anecdotal evidence suggests many people enter a cycle of homelessness, going from B+B, to the streets, to a friend's floor, then finding another B+B which is equally unsatisfactory. It is not uncommon for our clients to experience violence at some stage in this cycle. Most are black and are far more likely to be attacked on the 'homeless circuit'.
The Refugee Council

Difficulties have multiplied since February 1996 when access to benefits was stopped for many asylum seekers. Asylum seekers who make applications for asylum 'in-country' rather than at port, as well as those who have their applications refused and take their cases to appeal, are no longer eligible for a range of benefits including Income Support and Housing Benefit.[41] This means that unless a young person qualifies for assistance under the Children Act 1989 or community care legislation, they are likely to be destitute and entirely reliant on whatever charitable donations they can muster.

The Refugee Council reports that the main burden is being carried by refugee groups themselves, who are helping those who have no income by providing food and allowing them to sleep on floors. The Council reports that the *'poverty, stress and eventual squalor this creates can barely be imagined'*[41]... The hardship that has been caused is confirmed by a number of studies.[42] For example, one study finds that *'the withdrawal of benefit entitlement has caused intense hardship to asylum seekers and has been fraught with administrative problems,'*[43]

figure 25
ABDUL'S STORY

Abdul is a 16 year old boy from Iran. He entered the UK at one of the channel ports and made his way to London where he intended to lodge a claim for political asylum. He has no family, friends or contacts in the UK and so had nowhere to stay in London. He was clearly confused and disorientated when he arrived in London and this was exacerbated by the fact he spoke no English. He spent the first night sleeping rough on the banks of the Thames.

The following day Abdul was directed to the Refugee Council who, recognising his age and vulnerability, approached the local social services department. The Council was uncertain whether Abdul had slept on

'their patch' of the river and protracted negotiations took place between the Council and the Refugee Council before the matter was resolved and Abdul was placed with foster carers. Throughout these negotiations, Abdul was uncertain and anxious as to what would happen to him.

Approximately one week after being placed with foster parents Abdul turned 17 years and he was promptly moved from his placement to Bed and Breakfast accommodation.
(Abdul's story was provided by the Refugee Council)

YOUNG WOMEN

Women are also less likely to approach housing agencies, more likely to be living in hidden situations and more likely to be in a relatively weak economic position when it comes to searching for alternative accommodation.

It is, then, surprising to find that a relatively large proportion of young people who are sleeping rough are women. A 1991 Department of the Environment survey of single homeless people found that about a half of 16/17-year olds who were sleeping rough were women, this compared with a quarter of those between the ages of 16 and 24.[44]

This relatively new phenomenon is confirmed by agencies who submitted evidence to the inquiry. Many have reported increases in the number of very young women who are sleeping rough or living in other undesirable housing situations.

figure 26
YOUNG WOMEN AND HOMELESSNESS

A Shelter report on young women and homelessness says that women are less likely than men to approach housing and advice agencies. The shortage of hostel places for women and the hazards of sleeping rough, mean that they are more likely to stay with friends or relatives or endure difficult relationships.
Wherever I Lay My Hat: Young Women and Homelessness, Shelter 1991.

Interviews with 77 young homeless people, conducted for the inquiry, also found that women were reluctant to use traditional hostels because of stigma and fear.
Hearing Young People, CHAR, 1996

A survey of youth homelessness in Southampton in 1995 found that there was a ratio of 3 males for every 2 females, but amongst the youngest age group (15 to 17 years), there were as many females as males.
Evidence submitted to the inquiry

A survey of homeless young people in Birmingham, undertaken in 1993, found that homeless young women were younger on average than their male counterparts. Women made up 60% of all young homeless people between the ages of 21 and 25 years, but represented over two-thirds of those less than 21 years of age.
Young and Homeless in Birmingham, Barnardos Midlands, 1993.

A survey of young homeless people in Gloucestershire found that the proportion of females increased from 32% to 40% between 1993 and 1994/95. The proportion of females who were under 18 years of age also increased from 22% to 33% over the same period.
Finding the Right Combination: A report on young people's housing needs and provision in Gloucestershire 1994/95, Gloucestershire Forum for Young Single Homeless.

A survey of homeless 16 and 17 year olds undertaken in Croydon during March 1995 found that 57% were female.
A survey to Quantify and Qualify the Housing Situation of 16/17-year olds in the London Borough of Croydon, Croydon Under-18 Sub-group.

The majority of homeless 16 and 17 year old females have either left care or have left home because of abuse or neglect. Although they represent only a small proportion of all young homeless people, these young women are very vulnerable - they often have troubled pasts, are usually unprepared for independent living and many have to endure the difficulties and dangers of sleeping rough.

YOUNG LESBIANS AND GAY MEN

There is little research on the links between sexuality and homelessness, but the evidence that exists strongly suggests that lesbians and gay men are very vulnerable to homelessness. A number of agencies have reported to the inquiry that they see a significant number of young people who have become homeless because their sexuality has led to conflict, especially with their parents.

A report by the London Gay Teenager Group found that 11% of young lesbians and gay men were evicted by their parents when they told them about their sexuality. A survey of 4,000 callers to the London Lesbian and Gay Switchboard found that a quarter of callers had a housing problem directly related to their sexuality.
Almost half of those applying to Stonewall, a London housing association for young lesbians and gay men, said that harassment by landlords, neighbours and others was a factor in their homelessness.[46]

figure 27

NICKY'S STORY

I was working for the benefits agency in a northern city when the opportunity arose for my job to be transferred to London. When I arrived in London I had a job but no accommodation, and have had nine or ten addresses in the two and a half years I have been in London. I usually looked for accommodation in the Gay Press. I could afford to pay the rent on my salary, but found it difficult to come up with rent-in-advance and a deposit. I often stayed on friend's and friend's of friends floors for weeks at a time.

The accommodation I had before the last flat was a rented house in which the landlord lived. I was forced to leave there because he was beating up his girlfriend and I felt very unsafe. I had to leave at short notice and did not have the money for a deposit. I then sub-let a council flat - the tenant agreed I could have it for six months as he was going abroad. I received a call from the owner two months after moving in and he gave me 24 hours to leave the property. When I didn't leave the following day he became violent. He entered the flat while I was in work, he sprayed anti-gay graffiti on the front door and one evening he threw a canister of CS gas through the door.

I was in real danger and had to leave immediately. I went to an advice agency where there were many more people in my position and I didn't hold out much hope. I wrote to a large number of housing co-operatives but none responded. Eventually I was given Homeless Action's number and I now live in a shared house in South London.

Nicky aged 20

PART 1

Why we should care

We should care about youth homelessness because of the destructive effect the problem has on young people and the wider community.

The longer homelessness continues, the more likely it is that the physical and mental health of young people will deteriorate and they will become involved in drugs, heavy drinking, crime and prostitution.

With no or little income and no-one to support them, it is virtually impossible for young people to break out of their situation. In addition, the crisis-driven coping strategies that many young people adopt often multiply their problems in the longer term. The young person becomes a problem and the need for housing becomes a need for rehabilitation.

Although the negative effects of homelessness on young people are generally acknowledged, there is very little recognition of the impact of youth homelessness on society - this being less visible and difficult to measure. The inquiry found, however, that youth homelessness is costing the UK a considerable amount both socially and economically.

Calculations for the inquiry demonstrate that it is cheaper to rehouse young people than to ignore them until their needs and problems multiply, become problematic and require crisis intervention in the form, for example, of specialist care and extra policing.

The long-term consequences of continuing to ignore the needs of young people are even more disturbing. A number of independent sources have recently reported on a growing 'underclass' of poorly educated and untrained young people who are unemployed and living in poverty with few prospects for the future.

The generation gap is no longer about attitudes, but is about the 'haves' and 'have-nots'. The UK's social and economic well-being is seriously threatened when young people are not given real opportunities to become active and productive citizens.

THE EFFECTS ON YOUNG PEOPLE

LITTLE OR NO MONEY

We have already seen that unemployment amongst young people runs at roughly twice the national average - 16% compared with 8% across all age groups. Among young homeless people, however, the unemployment rate is considerably higher. **A number of surveys have found very high levels of unemployment amongst young homeless people with as many as 80% out of work.**

figure 28

YOUTH UNEMPLOYMENT: TWICE THE NATIONAL AVERAGE

- A national survey of single homeless people, undertaken in 1991, found that 80% of 16 to 24 year olds who were sleeping rough or living in bed and breakfast hotels or hostels were unemployed, and three quarters of these had been unemployed for 6 months or more.[1]
- In 1995 more than 80% of young homeless people in Hertfordshire were unemployed, although the unemployment rate for the county was only 11%.[2]
- Almost two thirds (64%) of clients of First Move, a project for young homeless people in Newcastle, were unemployed in 1995 and only 8% were on training schemes.[3]
- In 1995, 74% of young homeless people referred to St Basil's in Birmingham were unemployed.[4]

Once homeless, young people find it difficult to break out of the 'no home-no job-no home' cycle. There are many practical problems such as not having a permanent address and telephone, difficulties getting sufficient rest to be able to work properly and problems managing to appear presentable.

Being homeless saps energy as well as opportunities and, understandably, many young people in this position are unable to overcome the many practical difficulties that lie in the way of them finding and keeping a job or training place. There is also evidence that many employers are reluctant to employ young people once they realise that they are homeless.[5]

Young homeless people face considerable hurdles finding and keeping a job and even after they have housing their problems do not necessarily diminish. The rents charged for much temporary and supported accommodation are so high, often over £75 a week, that many young residents cannot afford to take up employment.

Without employment or a training scheme place, and with tight restrictions on their eligibility for benefit (see Section 2), many young homeless people find themselves with no or very little money.

For example, two-fifths (42%) of Centrepoint clients during 1995 had no income at all when they approached the agency.[6] Even when benefits are paid, they are simply too low to be able to support a young person who is living independently.

For example, a 16 or 17-year old living away from the parental home would receive around £28 a week or £4 a day. Inquiry members consider this to be significantly below a reasonable minimum.

Without money there is little prospect of many young homeless people being able to help themselves out of their predicament. The inquiry concludes that if the problems of poverty and homelessness continue there is a very real danger that the difficulties experienced by these young people will multiply and intensify.

It is common for the already limited accomodation options available to homeless young people to diminish even further over time. Friends and relatives no longer offer their sofas and spare beds, and if a young person is unable to return to the parental home and is unsupported by a statutory or voluntary agency, they become increasingly likely to be forced into rough sleeping. This can in turn lead to health problems, alcohol and drug misuse, petty crime and feelings of frustration and isolation.

HEALTH PROBLEMS

Although it is now generally recognised that homelessness and poor housing have detrimental effects on health,[7] it is less widely known that young homeless people, especially the very young, experience more health problems than their older counter-parts.

A Department of the Environment survey of single homeless people in 1991 found that 77% of 16/17-year olds reported at least one health problem compared with 54% of 18 to 24 year olds and 70% of all single homeless people.[1] Other surveys have found similarly high levels of poor health amongst young homeless people.

A National Children's Home survey of vulnerable young people living on their own[8] found that:

- A third had eaten only one meal or no meals at all during the previous 24 hours;
- Nearly all had unhealthy diets;
- A disproportionately high number had recently been physically ill;
- The overwhelming majority were depressed, worried or anxious.

As one would expect, health problems are most acute amongst young people who are sleeping rough. Young homeless people are not only more likely than average to have health problems, but when ill are also more likely to experience difficulties getting the care and treatment they need.

Access to primary and secondary health services is generally poor for homeless people, but evidence submitted to the inquiry suggests that the problem is even worse for young homeless people. Older homeless people are more likely to know their way around the system and to know where to go if they are unwell. Young homeless people, on the other hand, are often ignorant of the services available and how to gain access to them or are reluctant to make an approach.

The inquiry findings strongly indicate that there are growing numbers of young homeless people, especially amongst those sleeping rough and living in temporary accommodation, who suffer from depression, anxiety and mental health problems. This confounds the common assumption that mental illness is concentrated amongst older single homeless people, particularly those who have been discharged from psychiatric institutions.

Given the not uncommon combination of family abuse or neglect and homelessness, it is not surprising that a growing number of young homeless people, in particular the very young, have mental or emotional problems. In some cases these problems will have manifested themselves before the young person becomes homeless, while in other cases the additional burdens of homelessness may trigger the problems. **What is certain is that the hardships and stress of being without a permanent home will increase the likelihood of mental health problems developing and exacerbate any pre-existing problems.**

A survey undertaken by the Mental Health Foundation in 1995 (commissioned by the Department of Health)[9] confirms that there is a disturbingly high level of psychiatric disorders amongst young homeless people:

- a quarter had attempted suicide in the past year;
- more than a half had experienced severe parental neglect or abuse;
- they were twice as likely to suffer from psychiatric disorders as young people who were not homeless;
- in spite of the high incidence of mental health problems, the majority had not been diagnosed and of those that had only 15% had received treatment.

Other surveys have found similarly high levels of mental disorders amongst young homeless people.[10] It should also be noted that research has shown that chronic stress can pre-dispose someone to physical illness later in life.[11]

It is a cause of grave concern that most of these young people fall through the statutory safety nets and do not receive the help they need (see *Failure of the Welfare Safety Nets*, page 43).

Due to the lack of appropriate care and provision, an alarming number of young homeless people are ending up in psychiatric hospitals which are entirely inappropriate to their needs.
At a time when adult admissions to psychiatric hospitals are declining, the number of teenagers being admitted is actually increasing.

figure 29

INCREASED MENTAL HEALTH PROBLEMS AMONGST YOUNG HOMELESS PEOPLE

Our experience would suggest that there are growing numbers of young people in contact with homelessness agencies who exhibit some form of mental illness.

The Community Development Foundation

All housing agencies agree that they now have a higher percentage of young residents with mental health/personality disorders/learning difficulties and drug and alcohol related problems.

Key House Project, Bradford and North Yorks.

Around half the young people who use our services were the victims of abuse or neglect as children. These experiences mean that personality disorders and mental health problems (including alcohol and drug abuse) may develop and in many cases predate homelessness.

The London Connection Day Centre.

St Basil's has, since the early 1970's, expressed concern over young homeless people who are mentally ill. The situation has deteriorated over the last few years in the perception of our project managers. Frequently young people arrive at St Basil's without adequate assessment and/or social work support. They often consume enormous amounts of staff time and have great difficulty getting on with other residents, sometimes to the extent that they are rejected by those residents and driven out or leave of their own accord, with nowhere else to go.

St Basil's, Birmingham.

ALCOHOL AND DRUG MISUSE

There has been very little systematic research on the links between alcohol and drug use and homelessness amongst young people, although evidence submitted to the inquiry does suggest that there is a strong correlation.

figure 30

SUBSTANCE ABUSE AND HOMELESSNESS

- A survey of 505 drug misusing clients undertaken in October 1995 by Turning Point, the largest national charity helping people with drug, alcohol and mental health problems, found that over a third (34%) were homeless.[12]
- Over half (54%) of Turning Point's London clients in 1994/95 were homeless.[13]
- Research carried out for Turning Point's Hungerford project in 1995 found that only 17% of 837 young homeless people in the West End of London identified themselves as drug free.[14]

- Over a third (35%) of 77 young homeless people from 5 different locations across the country, who were interviewed about their experiences for the inquiry, said they were or had been dependent on drink or drugs.[15]
- During 1994/95, a quarter of young homeless people seen by the City Centre Initiative in Glasgow were using Class IV drugs and many others were using alcohol, other drugs or smoking heroin.[16]

The use of alcohol and other substances is common....all homeless people are exposed to the drug culture as part of their chaotic lifestyle. Drugs are used by young people both as part of their lifestyle and as a currency - a means of exchange and to generate finance.
St Anne's, Leeds

Drug use seems to be the norm amongst homeless young people in Central London.
Turning Point

Over the past three years youngsters have moved from alcohol, which is relatively expensive, to illegal drugs... This presents very real dangers, particularly when the habit is financed through prostitution, theft or exploitation.
Turning Point, West Midlands Project

Issues such as poor self-image, unemployment and homelessness are likely to have an effect on a person's drinking. Heavy drinking is common amongst homeless people generally, with evidence to suggest that up to half of rough sleepers are heavy drinkers. Given that up to one quarter of rough sleepers are under 25, it could be concluded that a fair proportion of young rough sleepers have an alcohol problem.
Alcohol Concern

There is good reason to believe that the incidence of drug and alcohol misuse amongst young people is widely and significantly under-reported. Turning Point says that it is rare for people under 18 years of age to acknowledge that their drug use is a problem for which they require help,[17] and worries about being stigmatised or prosecuted also lead many young people to conceal their drug-use.

In addition, many homeless projects refuse to accommodate people who take drugs, and so young people will understandably keep their drug taking covert in these circumstances.

It is difficult to pinpoint the precise causal relationships between homelessness and alcohol and drug misuse since there are often additional problems such as mental illness. However, it does appear that having a drug or drink problem can cause homelessness, and being homeless increases the likelihood of a young person becoming involved in drug and alcohol misuse.

It is relatively common for young people with alcohol/drug problems to have to leave the parental home. Drug or alcohol misuse and related problems are often the source of considerable friction between a young person and his/her parents.

If a young person is unable or unwilling to adjust their behaviour this often leads to them being ejected from the family home. Young people living independently can also lose accommodation because of their drug-use, or because of money problems resulting from their drug use.

Relations with parents and relatives can be adversely affected where a young person has an alcohol problem which might be affecting their behaviour. In the same way, where a parent or guardian has an alcohol problem this can lead to a breakdown in relations resulting in the young person striking out on their own.
Alcohol Concern

Young people who are homeless are more vulnerable to drug and alcohol misuse. Drugs appear to be readily available on the streets and in bed and breakfast hotels and hostels and drug misuse is part of the culture of the young homeless, helping to form bonds amongst peers. Drugs and alcohol can provide the means of escape from a troubled past and traumatic present.

Turning Point says that for many drug/alcohol use is a way of making life on the streets tolerable, helping to alleviate feelings of helplessness and hopelessness, creating a diversion from everyday boredom, and helping to pass the time of day. More worryingly, the charity also reports that *'many young homeless people have complex problems of which drug and alcohol use is often a symptom rather than a cause.'*[18]

Alcohol and drug use can create a number of problems for young homeless people. Just as alcohol/drug misuse can create homelessness, so it can make it difficult for young people to escape homelessness.

There are very few housing projects specifically for young people with alcohol or drug problems, and many general needs projects are reluctant to rehouse young people known to have a drug or alcohol problem. If a young person has drug related convictions they are likely to experience additional problems finding work and housing. If they do secure accommodation and still have a drug or alcohol problem, there is a very real risk that they might lose the accommodation because of their impaired ability to cope with the responsibilities of a tenancy.

Landlords and general housing providers will not accommodate young people who demonstrate drug/substance use, and most specialist projects for substance misuse are aimed at groups other than those who are in housing crisis.
St Anne's, Leeds

Those agencies providing support and help for people with drug problems have increasingly become aware that people with drug problems who are homeless or poorly housed are unlikely to be able to make significant changes in their drug-using behaviour.
Scottish Drugs Forum

Homelessness also compounds the health risks associated with drug and alcohol misuse. Homeless people often have a poor diet, they can be ill because of sleeping rough and they are liable to depression and poor mental health. Drug misuse can also lead to poor diet and physical stress and can have an impact on mental health.

When drug use and homelessness occur together the health risks are exacerbated and the health of young homeless people is almost certain to deteriorate. The Scottish Drugs Forum suggested that problem drug users who are homeless or in poor housing are also more prone to unsafe drug use, which in turn can lead to major health problems such as Hepatitis B, HIV, septicemia and overdose.[19]

ANTI-SOCIAL BEHAVIOUR AND CRIMINALISATION

There is no shortage of evidence which demonstrates the link between homelessness and offending, although here too there are uncertainties over the precise causal relationships in operation.

A study in 1993 by the Association of Chief Officers of Probation found that accommodation problems were judged by many young offenders to have had a significant impact on their lives, including offending behaviour.[20]

Moreover, it seems that offending becomes more likely the longer a young person is homeless, and that in many cases offending is just one of many problems (figure 31). Indeed, NACRO has expressed concern that young offenders often develop a *'chronic cyclical and repeating pattern of homelessness, offending and prison and homelessness.'* [20]

Once this pattern is established it becomes difficult to disentangle cause and effect, and to establish whether offending was mainly a consequence of homelessness or vice-versa. What is clear, however, is that homelessness can lead to offending, and young people are more likely to offend if they have multiple problems and/or have been homeless for a prolonged period.

figure 31
ANTI-SOCIAL BEHAVIOUR AMONGST YOUNG HOMELESS PEOPLE

- A Department of the Environment survey undertaken in 1992 found that 14% of young people had spent time in a young offenders' institution and 21% had been in prison or a remand centre.[21]
- 50% of young people referred to Stonham Housing Association during the first 6 months of 1995 had been in custody.[22]

- A survey of young homeless people in Merthyr Tydfil in South Wales found that 75% had been charged with an offence, nearly half had been remanded in custody and 20% had served a custodial sentence.[23]
- 31% of young homeless people seen by the City Centre Initiative in Glasgow during 1994/95 had been remanded in custody. In 1991/92 the proportion had been 21%.[24]

Although there is little research on the subject, it also appears that young homeless people, especially those who are misusing drugs or alcohol, run an increased risk of being drawn into prostitution. A number of organisations who work closely with young people have reported to the inquiry that a small minority of young homeless people, often with multiple problems, are turning to prostitution.

For example, the City Centre Initiative in Glasgow has reported that the proportion of young men it sees who are involved in prostitution has remained steady over recent years but the proportion of young women has doubled - from 7% in 1991/92 to 14% in 1994/95.[25]

However, we should not lose sight of the fact that the crimes committed by young homeless people tend to be anti-social - begging, soliciting, being drunk and disorderly - rather than serious. Young homeless people are also more likely to be the victims of crime than the perpetrators.

Evidence from recent research into crime and young homeless people suggests that the vast majority of offences are of the nuisance variety, including minor public disorder. They are also frequently drink related. Only a very small number of arrests are for serious crime. The majority of offenders are white, in the 20-25 age bracket, and male. They are often victims in their own right and are subject to robbery and serious assaults due to their vulnerability.

Baden Skitt, Assistant Commissioner, Metropolitan Police.

figure 32

YOUNG HOMELESS OFFENDERS

Statistics submitted to the Inquiry by Mid Glamorgan Probation Service show that, of all homeless offenders aged between 17 and 25 who pleaded or were found guilty during a six month period in 1995:

- A third had a drink problem;
- Two-fifths had a substance or drug problem;
- A third had problems with their family;
- A third had problems with money (mainly debts);
- Over two-thirds (67%) were considered to have a high risk of offending again.

FEELINGS OF FRUSTRATION AND ISOLATION

Young homeless people do not have the support and stability that young people need to thrive. Many have been rejected or mistreated by their families or have been in local authority care, and when they become homeless they already have a weak sense of their own worth.

Being homeless intensifies feelings of inadequacy, powerlessness, frustration and loneliness. With little or no money it is almost impossible for young people to find a way out of their predicament and if statutory and voluntary agencies are unable or unwilling to help, then a young person will understandably feel alone and frightened.

It would be wrong to suggest that all young homeless people experience health problems, and become involved in drug/alcohol misuse, prostitution and crime. However, **evidence points to a small but growing minority of young homeless people who have complex problems and needs and who are falling outside or through the welfare safety nets.**

These young people often have mental health or emotional problems, misuse drugs and alcohol, beg, steal and prostitute themselves and regularly experience violence and intimidation. Unless there is early intervention they are likely to bear the burden of these problems (for example, a criminal record, drug or alcohol problem, physical or mental illness) into later life.

The complexity of problems that people present with makes it difficult to know where to start. Young people often have a history of abuse and multiple placements in care. They cannot cope with life in hostels and hostels cannot cope with their needs. Instead, they sleep rough because they need the human contact and they take drugs to forget the pain of the past. Prostitution, drug and alcohol misuse, self-harm, offending and custody are all part of the pattern. Some of our young people feel they have been put here to be abused.
City Centre Initiative, which works with young homeless people on the streets of Glasgow

THE HIGH COST OF YOUTH HOMELESSNESS

The financial costs of youth homelessness are considerable, and increase the longer a young person remains homeless. Costs are incurred, for example, in terms of extra policing and increased health and social services care costs.

A cost benefit analysis, commissioned by the Inquiry, calculated that it may be considerably cheaper to prevent homelessness, through a more accessible, flexible and fairer Housing Benefit system for young people, than to bear the costs of them becoming homeless.

The model, described in more detail in Appendix 3, calculates the impact of potential homelessness on the financial flows associated with a young person who has no particular special needs.

It estimates the costs and benefits which accrue over a two-year period depending on whether a young person actually becomes homeless or whether support is provided in the form of Housing Benefit.

Two alternative scenarios are analysed. In the first, the young person does not become homeless; instead he or she obtains accommodation financed through Housing Benefit. Based upon assumptions about the likelihood that they obtain employment, and the wage that this provides, the financial implications both to the Government and society more generally (including the person concerned and the employer) are assessed. The second scenario examines the situation in which a young person is unable to find suitable accommodation and is forced to sleep rough for a period of one year when it is assumed that they return to their family.

Comparison of the model's middle-range scenarios suggests that the costs, both to society overall and to the tax-payer, are significantly lower where the young person receives Housing Benefit and does not become homeless.

Society benefits overall by around £2,200 during the two-year period when the person initially receives Housing Benefit. If, instead, the person becomes homeless there is a cost of about £5,600 over the period. **The net benefit to society of making Housing Benefit available to a potentially homeless young person is, therefore, around £7,800 over a two year period.**

If the question is viewed solely from the tax-payer's perspective the difference is smaller but still very significant. Costs to the tax-payer amount to £1,700 over two years if the person receives Housing Benefit, and £4,100 otherwise, a saving of around £2,400. In other words, **this analysis suggests that providing Housing Benefit in this situation actually reduces costs to the tax-payer by over 50% over a two year period.**

The savings outlined above are based solely on the financial costs of youth homelessness and take no account of the high human costs of homelessness both to young people themselves and the wider community. We have seen the devastating effects that homelessness can have on the lives of young people. If, knowing this, we chose to do nothing about the problem then we undermine the core values and principles of a civilized and humane society. Furthermore, we plant the seeds of future problems.

Only if young people have a positive belief in the future will they be inspired to become involved - to seek education, training and employment opportunities, to accept responsibility and to feel part of the local community. The situation for young people and how they view the future, should be matters of concern for the whole community.

PART 2

WHAT WE CAN DO

5 SOMETHING CAN BE DONE

6 PREVENTION

7 RESPONDING TO HOMELESSNESS

8 LOCAL STRATEGIES

9 A NATIONAL PRIORITY

Something can be done

Given the destructive effects of youth homelessness, in particular on the young people involved but also on the wider community, it is essential that a concerted and comprehensive effort is made to tackle the problem.

Much can be done to improve the situation without the injection of substantial new resources. However, just as there is no single cause of youth homelessness, so there is no single magical solution. A range of different initiatives are required to prevent homelessness and where homelessness is unavoidable to respond quickly and sensitively to the needs of young people.

Inquiry members were impressed by the imagination, energy and effectiveness of many local initiatives across the country. There is clearly much that can be learned from these schemes and wherever possible examples have been included in this part of the report (contact details are included at Appendix 4). We need a coordinated and holistic approach at both the national and local level to carry these diverse initiatives forward.

Housing, social, educational, training, employment and leisure services across both statutory and voluntary sectors need to work together in a unified framework to improve the life-chances of young people. In short, every area of the country should have a local strategy on youth homelessness. A local strategy not only represents the vehicle for driving preventative and remedial initiatives forward, but can also provide a tremendous spur to action.

Although it is difficult to pinpoint any single changes that would dramatically reduce the incidence of youth homelessness, policies aimed at reducing homelessness amongst young people leaving care and the restoration of welfare benefits to young people would have a significant impact on the problem.

Politicians and the public need to recognise that young people do not make themselves homeless on purpose. If there is a recognition of this and society provides care and support, accessible accommodation and benefits, it should never get as far as people sleeping rough.
Stonham Housing Association residents

The solution to youth homelessness begins with public and political recognition that there is a problem. Although policy makers, in national and local government, have a central

role to play, we cannot ignore the fact that youth homelessness is a social problem that often starts in the family home. It is there and in community locations, such as schools, youth clubs and religious groups, that preventative action must begin.

It is also essential that young people themselves are closely involved in the process of finding solutions. The great majority of young people do have the commitment, ability and perseverance to help themselves - witness the resolve and skill required to survive on the streets. However, given the harsh economic environment they face, most young people still require a helping hand during the transition to independence. In the case of young homeless people who are estranged from their parents and family, this assistance has to come from local statutory or voluntary agencies.

It is, nevertheless, important that young people are actively involved in sorting out their problems. The self-confidence, self-reliance and life skills required for adult life will only develop if young people are able to exercise more control over their lives and actively participate in building their own futures.

The inquiry has identified a range of different policies and initiatives, described here, which if implemented would significantly reduce the incidence of homelessness amongst young people.

Prevention is better than cure

Prevention is particularly important in respect of youth homelessness since, once homeless, young people find it difficult to find their way back to a stable housing situation. It may even be cheaper than a reactive approach, as our earlier analysis showed. It would certainly greatly reduce the enormous cost of human misery and thwarted potential that youth homelessness creates.

Young people have low priority for public housing and are usually priced out of private housing markets, especially if they are on benefits. It is, therefore, essential that every effort is made to prevent young people becoming homeless in the first place. Those who are thinking of leaving home should be made aware of the likely consequences and encouraged and supported to make adequate preparations.

Young people leaving local authority care are often multiply disadvantaged and so it is particularly important for them to receive the early support and preparation necessary to a successful transition to independence.

If the Housing Bill 1996 is enacted the right of vulnerable young homeless people to long-term housing will be removed: advice and prevention should therefore become far more important elements of local authority homelessness services. Indeed, the Bill intends to place a duty on local authorities to *'ensure that advice and information about homelessness and the prevention of homelessness, is available free of charge to any person in their district'* (Section 139 of the Housing Bill)

There are real opportunities here for local authorities to take their advice and assistance duties to 'non priority' applicants more seriously and provide services to young people that are relevant, accessible and comprehensive.

Although advice, support and education have important roles to play they will not, alone, solve the problem of youth homelessness. We have seen that 'structural' factors, such as unemployment and limited access to benefits and housing, have played a major part in the growth of youth homelessness and preventative strategies will only be effective if they include measures aimed at tackling these broader problems.

In spite of their evident good sense, preventative initiatives are thin on the ground. Most schemes and projects are aimed at young people once they have become homeless - few focus on early intervention to avert homelessness. Evidence to the inquiry suggests that preventative schemes can be particularly effective in the context of a wider strategy aimed at tackling youth homelessness. In this section, preventative schemes are considered under the following headings:

1. Education
2. Advice
3. Preparation and support for young people leaving care
4. Increasing housing opportunities
5. Increasing educational, training and employment opportunities
6. A benefits safety net
7. Family support

EDUCATION

Young people are generally ignorant of the realities of living independently and how difficult it can be to find suitable accommodation. Education programmes covering life skills and the issues of leaving home, housing and homelessness would help greatly. Sadly, few schools or youth clubs include them in their activities. Yet teachers are frequently the first people to observe that a young person may be at risk of homelessness.

The Government has supported the inclusion of projects on housing and homelessness in school curricula. The Homelessness Code of Guidance for local authorities states that *'education is crucial to help young people cope with independent living, and to ensure that they are aware of the risk of homelessness. Housing authorities should, therefore, liaise closely with education authorities to include projects on housing and homelessness in their curricula.'* [1]

In addition, the 1988 Education Act, which underpins the national curriculum, says that every pupil should receive an education which *'prepares them for the opportunities, responsibilities and experiences of adult life.'* It recommends that 14 to 16-year olds *'investigate the causes, benefits and disadvantages of leaving home... and identify and analyse the various options open to those who do so.'*

The inquiry recommends that all secondary schools and youth clubs introduce a programme of education on leaving home, housing options and life skills. Programmes should use eye-catching written material, new technology and involve local homeless and housing agencies to help get the message across. Young homeless people are actively involved in some education schemes (figure 33) and this peer-led approach should be used more widely. Information and advice delivered by other young people is more likely to be absorbed and the young homeless people involved also benefit from the experience.

Any education programme should include communication skills training. By teaching children and young people how to develop and sustain relationships it may be possible to improve family relations and make it easier for young people to seek help when they need it.

Teachers and youth workers should be trained to recognise and respond to signs that a child or young person is experiencing problems at home and may be at risk of becoming homeless. They should provide whatever support they can, but in most cases the child/young person will need to be put in touch with specialised agencies.

figure 33

EDUCATION INITIATIVES TO PREVENT YOUTH HOMELESSNESS

Norfolk Peer Education Project

This initiative was developed in partnership with Centrepoint's 'Leaving Home' Project which provides information for young people and helps teachers and youth workers prepare young people for leaving home. In 1994, Centrepoint helped to establish local partnership groups in six areas, including Norfolk. Organisations were encouraged to work together to identify gaps in leaving-home education in their area and devise new materials.

The Norfolk group includes youth workers, housing officers, hostel staff and volunteers. Centrepoint provided one day's training and the group subsequently identified three priority areas - peer education, a local data-base and the production of a video. Norfolk Youth and Community Service seconded a youth worker to the project who recruited young people for the peer education project. The young people involved have run activity and discussion sessions in schools and youth centres. These were very successful and repeat sessions have been requested. Each of the young people in the peer education project had a different experience of leaving home. A variety of different methods were used in sessions - for example, one member of the group designed a game to use with young people preparing to go to university.

The Norfolk project has been a considerable success. Although Centrepoint is no longer formally involved, the local group continues to flourish. Centrepoint plans to extend and develop peer education to cover other areas and groups - for example, African Caribbean and Asian young people, young women and young disabled people.

Schools Education Scheme, Yorkshire and Metropolitan Housing Foundation

Yorkshire and Metropolitan Housing Foundation, a charitable arm of Yorkshire and Metropolitan Housing Association, employs the country's first and only housing teacher.

Since its inception in 1992 the Foundation has provided a housing education service to over 60 secondary schools and colleges within Yorkshire, primarily with funding from Comic Relief as part of their youth homelessness initiative.

Providing skills and information to prepare for leaving home form the focus of this work and, although targeted at young people at risk of homelessness, the lesson content is relevant to all pupils. Emphasis has recently shifted towards the training of teachers and workers from relevant agencies, in order to make service delivery more effective and to reach greater numbers of young people.

To support this process, the Foundation has produced a housing resource pack which includes lesson plans, housing information, a pupil information pack and advice on how to build-up local information. The pack encourages teachers to introduce and develop housing and homelessness themes with 14 to 18-year olds, mainly within Personal and Social Education. A housing quiz on CD-ROM has been developed to complement the pack and to encourage active learning.

ADVICE

Timely and relevant advice is an important element of any preventative strategy. Given that young people are unlikely to be housed in the public sector, advice that can help them remain in their existing home or find something else that is suitable is particularly important.

Local authorities have a legal duty to provide 'appropriate advice and assistance' to homeless applicants that they do not accept for rehousing.[2] However, only a minority of authorities provide a comprehensive advice service tailored to the circumstances and needs of young homeless people.

In most areas the provision of advice is uneven and what is available is often provided by a patchwork of different statutory and voluntary agencies with different remits and client groups - for example, homeless projects, advice centres, local housing authorities, youth clubs and day centres.

figure 34

EARLY ADVICE AND SUPPORT TO YOUNG PEOPLE AT RISK OF HOMELESSNESS

Newcastle City Council

A study of housing applications in Newcastle in 1993 highlighted the fact that 88 of the 125 young people rehoused because of family breakdown in 1992/93 had previously applied for housing. As a consequence, the Council established an early warning and screening process for young people likely to become homeless.

In June 1993, First Move, a joint council and voluntary sector team set up to support young people, began to contact all those young people who had approached the local housing office to offer them advice and support. As a result, the number of young homeless people rehoused fell below 100 for the first time in ten years. Young people were diverted to other more appropriate options, including family reconciliation. The council concluded that this simple intervention had produced a significant change in both service use, and in the rehousing of the young homeless. [3]

Advice and information services to young people should be both comprehensive and accessible. Young people frequently have more than one problem (a common combination being homelessness, no or little income and family relationship problems) and, in addition, they often experience difficulties finding their way around the system to access the different types of information, help and advice they need.

Every town should have a well publicised place where young people can go for advice and help with problems relating to families, accommodation and benefits. It should be accessible and not bureaucratic or officious. Schools and colleges should know about it and should send people there.
Stonham Housing Association residents

Although research on the most effective way of providing young people with advice and information was not available to the inquiry there are some models that appear to be effective. The 'one-stop' shop, for example, provides young people with advice and assistance on a range of different issues in one place - see figure 35.

In some cases, these 'one-stop shops' cater specifically for young people and may include other facilities such as a drop-in centre. Out-reach services have also proved to be effective; taking advice and support out to young people who would otherwise be unlikely to seek help (for example, those sleeping rough and in bed and breakfast hotels). Mobile services have been used effectively in rural areas where the population is thinly distributed.

Advocacy work has an important role to play since many young people will need not just advice but also someone who will support and represent them during a particularly difficult time. They will need help to secure their full entitlement to benefits and to access housing, health and support services. In many cases young people find it less daunting to seek help on the telephone than in person, and so well publicised telephone advice lines should be considered.

Advice leaflets should be written specifically for young people and should cover a range of different issues, including benefits, training, employment and health as well as housing.
In some cases it will be useful to produce targeted leaflets for specific groups of young people - for example, those leaving prison, lesbians and gay men. With effective promotion and distribution, dedicated leaflets are more likely to reach their target audiences.

It is important to publicise advice services for young people in ways that will appeal directly to them. Services should be delivered from accessible, unintimidating locations - for example, young people are more likely to visit a shop-fronted property in the High Street than a second floor office in County Hall. Information should also be available at venues used by young people, such as bus and train stations, taxi firms and youth and community centres. For example, a purpose- built computer system, *'On the Right Track'* has been installed at Charing Cross station to give homeless people free information on where to find essential services in London.

figure 35

PRESENTING ADVICE TO YOUNG PEOPLE

The 'one-stop shop' approach - The HUB Centre in Bristol

The HUB Centre in Bristol, which opened in June 1995, has brought together six statutory and two voluntary organisations to provide a comprehensive range of services to people in housing crisis. It has a basic philosophy on choice, accessibility and confidentiality. Advisors from Bristol Cyrenians undertake initial interviews and people are then directed to health, employment, benefits, housing or social services staff, as appropriate. Further help from Avon Health Commission, employment/careers advisors and a Benefits Agency information officer is available within the same building. Housing services staff are able to deal with homeless and benefit applications and make referrals to the Council's rent deposit scheme. In addition, advice is also available from two Shelter Housing Advisors who are free to challenge any advice or decisions made by other HUB partners. The Centre believes that, given the all too common combination of benefit and housing problems, the involvement of the Benefits Agency has been crucial to its success to date.

A dedicated information leaflet - Rotherham Metropolitan Borough Council

A free, pocket-size, 26 page advice leaflet has been produced specifically for young people. It includes advice on housing, benefits, health, education, training, employment and also includes the contact details of a broad range of relevant organisations. Funded by Rotherham Metropolitan Borough Council, the leaflet was produced jointly by a number of local statutory and voluntary agencies which work with young people.

Out-Reach Advice - The City Centre Initiative in Glasgow

In 1990, the manager of Dunkin Donuts', a 24-hour fast food outlet in Glasgow city centre, approached the YMCA Glasgow concerned about the high numbers of young people using his premises at night. In response to his concerns, YMCA Glasgow appointed two youth out-reach workers to establish contact with vulnerable young people within Glasgow city centre and assess their needs for support services. Strathclyde Regional Council's Social Work Department and Community Education Service were at the time discussing the need for services for young people at risk within the city centre, while Glasgow Council for Single Homeless was campaigning for central advice and information services for homeless young people. In early 1991, the four agencies agreed on the need for a collaborative response and formed the City Centre Initiative.

The City Centre Initiative is a voluntary project which targets vulnerable groups of young people such as those sleeping rough, runaways and those involved in prostitution. Workers, operating in pairs, undertake streetworking five evenings a week between 5.00pm and 1.00am. Streetworkers' main functions involve:-

- *cold contacting young people not known to the project;*
- *maintaining and developing contact and relationships with existing contacts;*
- *providing crisis assistance on the streets;*
- *referring young people to CCI office services and other agencies where appropriate;*
- *liaising with other agencies offering direct services to homeless people on the streets at night.*

In addition to undertaking generalised streetwork with young people, two streetworkers are specifically responsible for identifying and responding to the needs of very vulnerable young women and men, in particular those involved in prostitution. In 1993 the City Centre Initiative extended its activities and established an office base to complement the work done by the streetworkers. In four years of operation the agency has had contact with 1,486 young people.

PREPARATION AND SUPPORT FOR YOUNG PEOPLE LEAVING CARE

A significant proportion of young people leaving foster or institutional care become homeless and it seems that one of the main reasons for this is that they receive insufficient support and are inadequately prepared for independence (see Part 1, Section 3). Leaving home is a difficult process for many young people but for care-leavers it can be especially hazardous.

They are very young (the great majority under 18 years of age) and vulnerable and do not have the option of returning 'home' should independence become too difficult. Given these substantial disadvantages, they need more support and preparation than other young people. Well in advance of leaving they should receive personal and life skills training. They should also be closely involved in the preparation of their care plan. The essential elements of any care plan are shown in figure 36.

In some cases, it may be appropriate for young people who are about to leave care to spend time in intermediate, semi-supported accommodation, although this should not be made compulsory. On leaving care young people must have safe and suitable accommodation to go to and must be provided with financial and other support to help them settle in.

Interviews with young people who have left care suggest that befriending schemes and the opportunity to return to a care-type situation during difficult periods would be of considerable benefit[4]. There are a number of possibilities for befriending schemes. Care workers could each be responsible for keeping in contact with one or a number of care-leavers and for providing on-going guidance and support. Or, young people who have already left care could befriend young people who are about to leave and offer friendship and support during the transition to independence and beyond.

A coordinated and planned approach should also be adopted for young people leaving offenders' and other institutions. There is growing evidence that young people leaving institutions, including prison, hospital and residential care, have a much higher than average risk of homelessness, and those who do not find suitable accommodation are more likely to return to institutional care.[5] One study has found that two-thirds of ex-prisoners who could not find a decent home re-offended within 12 months of release, compared with a quarter of those with good accommodation.[6]

Figure 36

ESSENTIAL ELEMENTS OF A CARE PLAN

1. A preliminary assessment of follow-on accommodation and support needs.
2. A 'through-care plan' which:
   - has as its over-riding objective, maintaining relationships which young people have built up with social workers, carers and others;
   - clarifies the objectives and responsibilities of social work staff and other agencies;
   - ensures the young person's access to the information, support and preparation that he or she requires to make a positive transition to independence;
   - identifies a key worker with overall responsibility for coordinating services, including follow-on accommodation, support and care management agencies;
   - draws together the potential contributions of housing departments, housing associations, community education, health and voluntary agencies.
3. Inter-authority cooperation to address the needs of young people who move between council areas.
4. Recognition that in the transition to adulthood young people will take risks, make mistakes and change their minds.
5. Consultation and involvement of young people.

(From Working with Young Homeless People, Part A, Guidance and Effective Action, Social Work Services Inspectorate, The Scottish Office, 1996.)

Figure 37

KEY FEATURES OF A THROUGH CARE STRATEGY

Without being unnecessarily prescriptive, it may be sensible to outline a number of features which should be apparent in a district-level 'through care' strategy. These would include:

1. A system which permits an overview of the support needs of all care-leavers and uses the information gleaned to develop practical initiatives.
2. Good forward planning in individual cases through the Child Care and Care Strategy reviews.
3. A range of 'through care' initiatives from the various units in the district (e.g. children's units, intermediate treatment, day care/IIT, foster care). Over and above individual support these might include:-
   - after care groups;
   - drop-in/contact initiatives;
   - volunteer/befriending schemes;
   - area team issue based groups and minimum support groups;

- emergency access accommodation;
- practical support on a range of things such as decorating, cooking, money;
- a range of supported accommodation and independent living resources;
- joint initiatives between the variety of child care resources within the district;
- good access to specialised programmes - e.g. supported employment, college courses, drug advice/rehabilitation schemes;
- regular dialogue with other departments and agencies on the needs of this group so that services become more responsive - for example, community education, housing, careers advice.

4. A tracking system to ensure that individual care plans are monitored and that there is a practical and flexible response to young people's changing needs and circumstances - including instances where a young person does not want the services available.
5. 'Through care' work should maximise opportunities for young people to participate in care planning.

Formulated by the former Strathclyde Regional Council and carried out by Glasgow City Council.

INCREASING HOUSING OPPORTUNITIES

Many young people have no option but to leave home, and when they do their housing options are generally very limited. Housing in the private and public sectors can and should be made more accessible to young people.

THE PRIVATE SECTOR

Given the difficulties that young people experience accessing decent quality private rented accommodation, there is a critically important role for agencies to act as intermediaries, providing young people with a helping hand into the sector. This assistance will become even more valuable after October 1996 when changes to the amount of Housing Benefit paid to under 25 year olds will make it harder still for them to afford private rented accommodation.

Agencies can help in a variety of different ways - for example, with advice, rent in advance and bond payments, a register of approved landlords and properties, a supported lodging scheme or a nominated referral scheme (figure 38). The most enduring and productive schemes are those that are run jointly or in close cooperation with private landlords and where both landlords and young people benefit from the arrangement.

Agencies can improve their contacts with landlords (through, for example, local forums or consultative committees), offer support to landlords and strengthen their negotiating position by offering landlords something in return for their cooperation - for example, the speedier handling of Housing Benefit claims, improvement grants, support to tenants, sensitive referrals or housing management services. The London Borough of Ealing, for example, fast tracks the Housing Benefit claims of non-priority single homeless people living in bed and breakfast accommodation owned by approved landlords.

However, this cooperative approach will only be effective if different council departments and agencies have shared objectives and a common approach. It is no good local authority environmental health and housing benefit departments taking a rigid regulatory approach when other departments and agencies are attempting to foster mutual trust and cooperation.

Supported lodgings can be a particularly important resource for 16/17-year olds, especially if this type of accommodation is secured before there is time for the homeless label to stick. If 16/17-year olds had access to benefits supported lodgings could become even more important providing young people with the support they need within their own communities.

There is clearly considerable scope for agencies to do more to help young people secure privately rented accommodation. The desperate shortage of long term accommodation must not, however, lead to agencies using accommodation that is unsuitable (for example, bed and breakfast accommodation) or rehousing vulnerable young people without the support they need.

It is cruel to dump homeless young people in bed and breakfast hotels or run down bedsits with no-one to care about and support them. Many young people living in these conditions do not eat properly and become ill. They suffer psychological ill effects because of loneliness and are more likely to be drawn into crime and drugs when they are isolated.
Stonham Housing Association residents.

Labour mobility is essential to the economy. At the top end of the jobs market mobility is encouraged by relocation packages, including mortgage subsidies and moving expenses. There is no equivalent for unskilled and semi-skilled labour, however, and it is at the lower end of the employment market that housing and mobility opportunities are most constrained.Medium to large sized companies should consider providing employees with grants or loans to help them cover the expenses of moving and securing suitable accommodation.

figure 38

USING THE PRIVATE SECTOR

Supported Lodgings Scheme - NACRO

The aim of a scheme of this type is to recruit and support a network of local people who can offer a room in their home to a homeless person. There are minimum standards covering furniture, heating, access, food, support, confidentiality and equal opportunities. Householders are vetted and the needs and requirements of both parties are carefully matched.

The tenant and householder are required to sign a contract setting out the rights and responsibilities of both parties. Typical tenants are aged 16 years or more and have recently left home or institutional care and are inadequately prepared for independence. It may also be a suitable form of accommodation for people with mild learning difficulties, mental health problems and/or those who are under stress.

Schemes can offer different levels of support. - for example, acting as a broker between potential tenants and private landlords, withdrawing support once the tenant is settled in the self-contained property.

NACRO runs supported accommodation schemes in Essex, Lincolnshire, Cheshire, Greater Manchester and South Wales.

Rent Deposit Scheme - East London Homelink (Quaker Social Action)

East London Homelink identifies single unemployed people living in hostels and other temporary accommodation who would like to move into the private sector and then finds suitable properties. On acceptance, a month's rent-in-advance payment is made which is recouped from Housing Benefit.

A guarantee is issued enabling the landlord to claim up to an agreed amount against theft or damage. Careful matching and extensive support has meant that over 90% of tenants renew their tenancies after 6 months and cash losses are below 2% of the sums guaranteed. About 180 tenancies are created a year, around 50 of these to African refugees. Resettlement support is provided by 30 trained and supervised volunteers.

Nominated Tenancy Scheme - Derby City Council

Derby City Council offers landlords discretionary or enhanced renovation grants for improving or converting empty or run-down properties to provide rented housing. One scheme, Rented Accommodation for Single people (RASP), is specifically for young single people. HMO landlords receive enhanced renovation grants in return for providing good quality rented accommodation to young single people nominated by the council. The amount of grant is usually around £3,000-£3,500 per home up to a maximum of 75% of the works and is calculated according to property type, the number of homes provided and the landlord's financial circumstances.

THE PUBLIC AND VOLUNTARY SECTORS

Although not a traditional provider of housing for young single people, the public sector is an increasingly important accommodation source. The more difficult it becomes for young people to afford housing in the private sector, the more likely it is that they will turn to councils and housing associations for accommodation. Part 1 demonstrated how the number of single applicants to councils has increased dramatically over recent years.

Although families with dependent children will continue to be a priority for rehousing, it is essential that councils and housing associations do all they can to increase access for young single people. **Councils and associations should review their waiting list and allocations policies to ensure that there are no unnecessary barriers to young people, such as age or residency qualifications.** Many councils and associations will not rehouse 16/17-year olds on legal grounds, and some will not even accommodate young people under the age of 21 years. However, recent guidance from the Welsh Federation of Housing Associations[7] - suggests that landlords can safely let properties to under 18 year olds using a license agreement.

The inquiry acknowledges that councils and associations do sometimes experience management difficulties when they rehouse young single people, but evidence suggests that this is usually because young people are rehoused in poor quality accommodation, away from family and friends, and with no or little support or supervision.

Given their vulnerability, it is essential that young people are rehoused in decent quality accommodation, close to the people they know and with the support they need. Some local authorities and housing associations treat applications from the sons and daughters of tenants sympathetically in recognition, for example, of the importance of strengthening local communities.

The importance of providing on-going support to young vulnerable people once they have been rehoused is discussed in more detail in the section *Responding to Homelessness* on page 111.

Poor accommodation seems to go hand in hand with street crime, boarded up properties, violence, illegal money lending and substance abuse. Recently, a young homeless person was rehoused in a street where only one other property was occupied. Gangs of young people intimidated our client to the extent that he was unwilling to leave his flat, his sleep was continuously disrupted which affected his health and ability to continue on his training course. When he did go out, on reaching the end of his road he would run to his door rather than walk. What quality of life has he?
St Anne's, Leeds

Councils and housing associations should consider providing shared and furnished accommodation. Although most young people have a long-term preference for self-contained accommodation,[8] shared accommodation is often cheaper, more sociable and allows for a gradual

adjustment to independent living. Research by the Priority Estates Project has shown that shared accommodation schemes work best if the units are small (two or three people) and there are resident and caretaking staff to provide supervision and support.[9]

There are a range of different models for the provision of shared accommodation, for example shared houses or self-contained clustered accommodation with some communal areas and facilities, and so agencies should investigate the appropriateness of different types before providing shared accommodation.

If a young person is unable to furnish and equip their new home they are unlikely to remain there; yet an unfortunately large proportion of young people find it difficult to obtain even the most basic items. As mentioned in Part 1 young people are not usually a priority for Social Fund loans and if estranged from their family they are unlikely to receive help from that source.

Given the importance of furniture in determining how well a young person settles into their new home, **agencies should consider offering accommodation on a furnished or semi-furnished basis and establishing a furniture store to help those in unfurnished accommodation.** Newcastle City Council's furniture scheme (figure 39) was introduced in response to the inability of young people to furnish their homes and the consequent impact this had on their stability as tenants. The housing department monitored tenancy length for 8 years and during that period the average life of all young people's tenancies was 36 weeks. However, between 1988 (when single payments were abolished) and 1991 (when the council introduced its furniture scheme) the average length of tenancy for young people reduced to 29 weeks.

Where councils and associations have low demand properties, they should consider improving and redesignating them for use by young single people. For example, high rise blocks of flats and low demand sheltered schemes have been successfully remodeled and allocated to young single people. Northern Counties Housing Association, for example, is converting a former old people's home in Sheffield into a 60 bed foyer for young people.

A survey undertaken in 1995 found that 92% of councils and 79% of housing associations had 'difficult-to-let' sheltered housing for elderly people and that the problem was 'serious and widespread.'[10] Schemes were 'difficult-to-let' mainly because of their design (many consist of bedsits with some communal facilities) and more generally because the demand for sheltered accommodation has waned over recent years.

There is clearly considerable potential for some of these schemes to be redesignated for use by single people. Indeed, in May 1996, the Department of the Environment said it would be taking *'positive steps to encourage the conversion of bedsits provided for elderly people either to more suitable accommodation for them or, while protecting the interests of elderly people, to alternative uses such as accommodation for young single people.'*[11]

However, it is essential that improvements and conversions are not done on the cheap and that schemes are closely managed on completion. If young single people are rehoused in poor quality accommodation with no or little support and supervision, problems are bound to arise for the landlord, young tenants and neighbours alike.

Although it is now fairly widely recognised that high rents create a poverty trap for many tenants, making it uneconomic for them to work, the problem is less often linked with public and voluntary sector housing. However, **the rents of many housing association properties and voluntary sector temporary and supported housing schemes are well above affordability levels.**

For example, average rents in London hostels for 16 year olds, even with any discounts for those working, are in excess of £70 for lodgings only and can reach £120 a week.[12] The foyer movement is sensitive to the affordability issue and has made every effort to keep rents to the minimum that funding will allow, but the average foyer rent was nevertheless around £76 a week in 1995.[13]

High rents mean that many young people living in housing association properties and voluntary sector schemes have no incentive to find work since the low pay they are likely to receive, should they find a job, would not cover the rent and service charges payable. In addition, Housing Benefit ceilings set by local authorities do not always match the rents that landlords charge, which means that many homeless people are financially worse off once they are rehoused. For example, a half of the homeless people rehoused through the Rough Sleepers Initiative said they were financially worse off following rehousing[14].

The gap between the rent payable and Housing Benefit received is likely to increase significantly for under 25 year olds from October 1996 when new Housing Benefit limits are introduced. This will cause shortfalls for many young people which will absorb most of their disposable income.

Although high public and voluntary sector rents are a consequence of national housing and rent policies, there is still much that can be done at the local level to minimise the problem. Allocations need to be made sensitively and young people encouraged to claim the benefits they are entitled to. Agencies should also ensure that young people who no longer need expensive supported accommodation are moved into more affordable, longer term accommodation as soon as possible.

The wages and benefit systems currently interact to provide little incentive for young people to work; while the housing system provides little support to move to where employment is available. Unless action is taken matters will almost certainly deteriorate further particularly for young people.
The Foyers Federation

Over 95% of young people in homeless establishments are unemployed. This is partly due to their homeless situation and the difficulty in maintaining employment. It is exacerbated by a funding system in supported accommodation that is either inflexible in the case of registered accommodation or structurally unworkable in the case of unregistered accommodation. Supported accommodation funding needs to be reviewed to take account of the importance of fostering employment opportunities.
Strathclyde Regional Council

figure 39

USING THE PUBLIC SECTOR - NEWCASTLE CITY COUNCIL FURNITURE SCHEME

Newcastle City Council currently maintains approximately 3,000 furnished tenancies in flats and houses distributed throughout the city. The service is widely advertised and is open to a general waiting list, homeless and special needs applicants.

The Furniture service is self-financed from a service charge added to the rent. There has been an overwhelming preference for 'part-furnished' tenancies, providing a limited range of high quality goods such as a cooker, beds and cabinet furniture. Fully furnished units are available but are declining in importance.

The furnished tenancies have been shown to increase the length of tenancies overall, to reduce tenancy abandonments, and to increase the comfort and satisfaction resulting from rehousing. There is some evidence that there are reduced debts related to establishing a home.

INCREASING EDUCATIONAL, TRAINING AND EMPLOYMENT OPPORTUNITIES

There is a clear link between unemployment, poverty and homelessness and so one of the most effective long-term preventative strategies is to help young people into education, training and decently paid employment.

The Government recognises that there is a pressing need to raise the basic and vocational skills of young people in this country, and has supported schemes which tackle the twin problems of homelessness and unemployment. For example, the Single Regeneration Budget is an important mechanism for coordinating employment and housing strategies at the regional level. The Government has also supported other initiatives, such as homeless job clubs and customised training, which have successfully increased the employment opportunities of young people.

However, we saw in Part 1 that youth training (YT), which is the only form of training available to the great majority of 16/17-year olds, is failing to help those in most need. There is evidence of a growing minority of young people who are poorly educated and trained and whose prospects for the future are disturbingly bleak.

There is a pressing need to find more effective ways of helping young people into education, training and employment. Although it is beyond the remit of this report to recommend a comprehensive strategy on employment and training, these issues clearly are key determinants of young people's life chances including the type of housing they are able to secure. The inquiry has therefore outlined below a number of initiatives it believes should be considered further.

Encouragingly, agencies who work with young people are increasingly aware of the relationship between homelessness and unemployment; a number of initiatives which simultaneously tackle both problems have recently been developed. For example, since 1992 around 40 foyers have been developed, borrowing on the concept of the French *foyers pour jeunes travailleurs*. These provide young people with hostel-type accommodation, training, support and job-search facilities.

Foyer schemes currently provide some 2,000 bedspaces, and a further 30 or so foyer initiatives are in the pipeline.[13] Foyers represent an important resource, providing young people with the stable and supportive environment needed for them to be able to make the most of educational, training and employment opportunities. A recent evaluation of foyers, undertaken for the Foyers Federation, found that around a half of foyer residents find jobs and that 70% of these jobs are full-time.[13]

The foyer initiative should, however, be developed flexibly and in conjunction with other housing and employment initiatives for young people. We have seen that young people's needs circumstances and aspirations vary, as do local employment and housing conditions, and so a range of different responses is usually required. There are encouraging signs that the foyer concept is being adapted to local circumstances and needs. For example, in rural areas where large, centralised foyers would be inappropriate, a number of small, dispersed and mobile schemes have been developed (see the example of the Richmond, North Yorkshire YMCA scheme, figure 42).

It should also be remembered that foyers provide accommodation and support over a relatively short period of time and young people will need help to find more permanent accommodation and may also need follow-up help with training or employment.

Many housing and employment initiatives are targeted at young people when they are homeless or threatened with homelessness. The inquiry found that, although these schemes have an important role to play, early intervention is also required to help young people into work and housing and to prevent homelessness from occurring in the first place.

A growing number of young people need relatively intensive pre-vocational training and do not fully benefit from many employment and training initiatives. Foyers and other agencies which deal with young homeless people have found that many young people they see need very basic training covering the sorts of skills (for example, literacy, numeracy and basic life and social skills) which most young people learn at an early stage from school, parents or friends.

Although the recent evaluation of foyers clearly highlights the lack of soft skills amongst young people as an issue of national importance, with an average staff/resident ratio of 15:1 and the emphasis placed on output measures by funders[13], there are serious concerns over the capacity of the foyer movement to provide the types of intensive support required. The inquiry points to a wider availability of basic pre-vocational support and training for young people through schemes like the Bristol Cyrenians Scheme, described in figure 42, which complements the work done by a local foyer.

Many young homeless people also need relatively intensive support to help them find work. *'Off the Streets and into Work'* is an innovative four-year project aimed at providing skill development, training and jobs for 15,000 single homeless people in Central London. It is the first attempt to provide a coordinated service and is described in more detail in figure 42.

Although there is growing recognition of the need of many young homeless people for relatively intensive levels of support and training, there is little evidence on what works best. **The inquiry believes that there should be an investigation into the most effective ways of bringing young people up to a minimum pre-vocational standard and of helping more needy young people into employment.**

It may be that we could learn from schemes designed for other vulnerable groups. For example, the 'training-in-systematic-instruction' (TSI) method, which has been sponsored by the Joseph Rowntree Foundation, has been used very effectively with people with learning difficulties. The scheme trains people for 'real' jobs. A trainer helps a client find a job, learns the job her or himself, trains the client to do the job and then supports the client in the job until she/he can cope alone

There is a growing recognition of the contribution that non-market forms of work including caring, volunteering, self-help and local economic trading schemes (which use non-monetary units to exchange labour services amongst members), can make to the development of skills and community well-being.[15]

Indeed, young people are more likely than older people to be involved in voluntary work,[16] and a number of organisations who submitted evidence to the inquiry said that the experience of homelessness leads many young homeless people to go on to volunteer.

figure 40

ANDREW'S STORY

I became homeless in 1991 when I was released from prison. My probation officer gave me no support and for 4 years I moved from hostel to hostel. In 1992 I found out I was HIV-positive and as a result was kicked out of the hostel I was staying in. I then felt I was hopeless and worthless until I heard about the Centrepoint Intake and thought I could make something of my life if I had a bit of support.

I was accepted into the hostel in August 1995. Since then I have become a volunteer for prisoners with HIV. I write to them at least once a week. I also do painting and decorating. I am waiting to move into my own flat. I now have regular contact with my Dad and the Salvation Army are looking for my real mum. Once I settle into my new flat I want to work with people who are HIV and are homeless. I found that when I was homeless not many people wanted to help me. I am now able to feel relaxed and talk over my fears.

Some self-help schemes, for example, not only develop the skills and experience of young people but also provide them with housing. **Self-build projects** involve a group of young people building their own homes, which they usually rent from an authority or housing association. Not only do such projects produce much needed housing, but they also provide young people with opportunities to be involved in decision making processes, work cooperatively and develop building skills.

Participants also grow in confidence and develop social skills that are useful to them more generally. There is evidence that participation in self-build can achieve a lasting change in young people's circumstances - for example, young people usually remain settled in their accommodation for many years and many find employment following completion of the scheme (see John's story, figure 41). In spite of the obvious advantages of self-build, schemes can be time-consuming and funding is uncertain.

Other self-help schemes involve young people improving and decorating run-down properties which they then move into, sometimes on a shared basis. These schemes have many advantages: they bring empty properties back into use; they improve local housing conditions; they can be very cost effective in areas of low property values; they provide young people with accommodation; and they also develop the skills and experience of the young people involved. Both a community self-build and renovation project are described in figure 42.

figure 41
JOHN'S STORY

For John, growing up was a painful process. Things were not going well at home and at nineteen his parents threw him out. His first taste of independence was bed and breakfast which he describes as 'a hell-hole'. Then he moved into a small hostel where he received support to go on a business course but still he could not find a job.

As this was temporary accommodation he was also concerned about how long he could stay there. Then he was put in touch with the Community Self-Build Agency which was recruiting young people to join a self-build scheme. This meant spending one day a week in a training centre and four days a week actually building his own home.

Since joining the project he has earned the respect of his parents and they are now in regular contact. John and eleven other young people moved into their block of flats last year. On the strength of his experience and commitment John has been offered a job as a trainee in a surveyor's office. As John puts it, "It's like a dream come true. With a home and a job, what else do you need in life?"

Case study provided by the Community Self-Build Agency

There is potential for public organisations to do more to create training and employment opportunities for young people. A number of housing associations, for example, have been actively involved in employment and training initiatives in an attempt to get added value from their investments and to promote local community interests.

For example, South London Family Housing Association has its own building firm which aims to be self-financing . Many associations now include clauses in large building contracts setting out a minimum percentage of local people to be employed on a scheme and the training packages to be provided.

However, there can be difficulties with these schemes. The construction industry is a harsh environment within which to create jobs. Recent research has shown that the number of jobs and training places generated is modest and that any positive impacts tend to be short-term with many people returning to unemployment.[17]

At the same time that recognition of the need for community-based initiatives has grown, pressures for value-for-money and volume building have restricted the potential for innovative non-housing activities.[17] In spite of these constraints, housing providers can still do much to enhance the training and employment opportunities of young people through, for example, urban regeneration initiatives.[18]

figure 42
SELF-HELP SCHEMES

The Gateway Project

Opened in 1993, the Gateway Project in Southwark is a purpose-built housing and training centre for young single homeless people in London. It caters for up to 116 short-term residents, and in addition has 64 units of permanent accommodation. The project aims to provide young people between the ages of 18 and 25 with a secure home-base and the necessary skills and experience to maximise their personal and employment potential enabling them to move on to employment opportunities, training, education and preparation for work.

Young people are referred by a number of agencies and a proportion by the Clearing House, a project developed under the Rough Sleepers Initiative. Lookahead Housing Association and the Peabody Trust provide the accommodation, whilst the Grandmet Trust and London Enterprise Agency provide access to employment training, work experience and related skills training. In the first year, 127 young people found employment and 38 moved into independent accommodation. The Project, which is run on a partnership basis, believes that the key to its success has been its emphasis on one-to-one counselling and guidance. The two most important difficulties for the project to date have been the uncertainties over long-term funding and the shortage of longer-term move-on accommodation.

The Richmond Foyer, North Yorkshire

The Richmond Foyer was established in January 1995 to meet the varied needs of young people approaching the Richmond YMCA. For some young people, housing and benefit advice is all the help they need but many others require more intensive support, including help to find training and employment.

The foyers concept was applied because of its emphasis on a supportive environment and integrated services, but schemes were tailored to suit local circumstances and needs. The YMCA decided against large scale hostel type accommodation because it would have involved young people moving away from their home areas and would have had less local support.

Instead, the YMCA has developed two houses providing 9 bed-spaces and a mobile service which can reach young people in the more isolated areas of North Yorkshire. Support, training, social and other services are provided from the Richmond YMCA which has the advantage that young people who are not resident at either the hostel or foyer houses can use the service.

The YMCA has very close links with other local agencies, some of whom are represented on the Foyer Steering Group, and will refer young people on for more specialised training and support as required. To date, move-on accommodation has been provided in the private sector - young people are encouraged to join the Bond Saving Scheme as soon as they join the foyer. However, a local housing association is developing permanent housing scheme for young people and the foyer will have nomination rights to some of the properties. The mobile service operates from a transit van which is equipped as an office.

Young people in the most isolated areas experience considerable problems getting the help and advice they need and so the mobile service has been particularly useful. The foyer has accommodated around 20 young people since it opened in January 1995, but very many more young people have received advice, training and support. For example, from January to March 1996, the foyer helped 28 young people.

Foundation Skills Training, Bristol Cyrenians

In September 1995, Bristol Cyrenians employed a skills and learning development worker to work specifically with homeless clients to help them build up the core skills, such as literacy, numeracy, self-confidence and social skills, required for them to be able to take up educational or training courses or employment.

The post, which is funded for three years by the Harry Crook Foundation, was established because many of the young people Bristol Cyrenians are in contact with lack very basic skills and the experience of homelessness further erodes their self-confidence.

Jan Andrews, the training officer, says that the experience of homelessness de-skills and devalues people and that many homeless people consequently need a lot of support, often on a one-to-one basis, before they can go on to take up employment or other forms of education or training. Since taking up her post 9 months ago, she has worked with around 70 homeless people the majority of whom are under 30 years of age. She provides core skills training either in one-to-one or workshop sessions and also refers people on to other courses such as Training for Work or open learning courses, as appropriate. She will soon start to

provide units from the Foundation Training Award programme - accredited by the Award Scheme and Accreditation Network - which has also provided accredited core training courses for the Big Issue and the London Connection day centre.

Community Service Volunteers

Community Service Volunteers (CSV), the national volunteer agency involves young homeless people as volunteers through its National Network and Local Action schemes.

CSV specifically targets the involvement of young homeless people as volunteers through two Local Action projects in London and Glasgow. Homeless young people are referred by local networks, statutory and voluntary agencies, to volunteer part or full-time on individually tailored placements with people in need. Volunteering in itself is not the answer to youth homelessness, but it offers a positive experience for the young people involved. CSV Local Action provides young people who face difficulties themselves with the opportunity to become givers rather than receivers of care. Placements are structured and supported, and can be a starting point for moving to a job, training or further education. Whatever they move on to do after their placement, CSV volunteers gain new skills, self-esteem and confidence from making a contribution valued by the people they help.

Off the Streets and into Work

This initiative aims to provide skills development, training and jobs for some 15,000 single homeless people in Central London over four years. It is funded by the Single Regeneration Budget, European Social Fund, training and enterprise councils (TECS), local authorities, charitable trusts and the business sector. A partnership with representatives from the private, public and voluntary sectors oversees the project's development with CENTEC, Homeless Network and Westminster City Council as core members.

There are four elements to Off the Streets:-

1. **Streets Ahead Employment Agency** - *based opposite Holborn Station, this is the first employment agency for homeless people and is run by the Peabody Trust and Centrepoint. It was opened in March 1996 and will eventually provide short-term or permanent employment for hundreds of homeless people.*

2. **Vocational Guidance Teams** - *are run by London Connection (under 25s) and St Mungo's Association (over 25's) supported by the Careers Service Partnership. They provide advice and careers counselling to clients and are establishing a system of outreach clinics to reach a wide number of people*

3. **Skills and job training provision** - *is being offered by 6 agencies who provide a range of different services, from training in basic skills, confidence building and job readiness to job specific skills in the fields of IT, retail, hotel and catering. It is anticipated that more skills areas will be added as the project progresses.*

4. **Training for staff in homeless agencies** - *ensures that key workers encourage homeless people to visit a guidance team, and provide informal back-up as clients undertake training or work.*

Community Campus

Community Campus is a cooperative which was formed in 1987 in response to the deepening housing crisis facing young people in Cleveland. The project provides accommodation and support for around 80 young people in housing need across Middlesborough and Stockton. The emphasis is very much on tenant participation. As well as regular tenants meetings and training events, the project holds outward-bound events, runs a football team, organises regular rambles and hosts numerous fundraising events. The high level of tenant involvement in the project is reflected in the high numbers of tenants and ex-tenants who are company members and are represented on the committee of management.

In 1991, in partnership with Jarvis Training Management, Community campus set up Key Skills to improve empty houses and provide training and housing for young people. Young people renovate and decorate empty properties purchased by the project and have first refusal on the tenancies.

Since its inception the scheme has created 25 units of accommodation in 10 renovated properties with further units in the pipe-line. All rental income is ploughed back into the scheme for the purchase and renovation of further properties. The project provides skills training towards NVQ Level 2 in general building operatives, painting and decorating, carpentry and joinery and bricklaying. To date some 70 young people have gone through the programme.

The scheme is very cost effective since unimproved properties can be purchased for as little as £12,000 to £15,000 and renovated for around £6,000. This means that 3 or 4 young people can be rehoused for as little as £20,000 and receive training as part of the package. The scheme has attracted considerable interest and is already being replicated in other areas of the country.

North Tyneside Youth Self-Build Scheme

This self-build scheme, which was initiated by a group of young homeless people, has created 8 houses on what was a derelict site in North Tyneside. The young people began to explore the feasibility of building their own homes in 1989 and by early 1993 they had secured funding and work had started on site.
By July 1994, some 17 months later, they had moved into their new homes.

North British Housing Association acted as development agent for the scheme and, in return for their labour, each young person owns a 25% stake in their home and pays rent on the remainder. All members of the group have received National Vocational Qualification training to level 1/2 and, in spite of very high local unemployment, by August 1994 six of the eight were already in work.

A BENEFITS SAFETY NET

The inquiry believes that one of the changes that would have the greatest impact on youth homelessness is the restoration of benefits to 16 to 24-year olds.

In Part 1 (Section 2) we saw that the withdrawal and reduction in benefits paid to young people have greatly increased the financial pressures on families (where young people are still living at home) and made it more difficult for young people to afford alternative accommodation.

The inquiry accepts that it may be difficult to restore benefits immediately. However, the savings made from preventing homelessness would go some way to covering the additional costs in benefits - see appendix 3.

Youthaid has calculated that at any one time during 1993/94 there were on average 117,000 unemployed young people without an income and that the cost of restoring an Income Support safety net (at 1994/95) rates would be £167.3m per year[19].

Although there are strong moral and financial reasons for restoring benefits to young people, the inquiry accepts that this may not be possible in the immediate future, and therefore proposes a number of smaller scale changes to benefit rules (see Recommendations on page 109) which would significantly improve the situation of many young people. For example, given the dangers and difficulties experienced by many 16/17-year olds who are living away from home, the inquiry believes that there should be a right of appeal against decisions regarding severe hardship payments. Also, the 16-hour rule which means that a young person who is on an educational course of more than 16 hours a week is disqualified from benefit, should either be abolished or revised to extend the permissible period.

The fact that young people are less likely than average to claim and receive the benefits they are entitled to is a cause for considerable concern.[26] Under claiming is probably a consequence of several factors, including: young people not knowing their way around 'the system' or what benefit they are entitled to; a lack of confidence; and services that are not open or friendly to young applicants. The eligibility of applicants is of little consequence if services are so impenetrable that many young people who are eligible do not bother to apply. Malcolm's story in figure 43, highlights the problems that young people can encounter. Advice and information to young people on the benefits they might be eligible for should be clear, accessible and made widely available.

As well as recommending a number of detailed changes to the benefit eligibility rules, the inquiry strongly urges the Government to review their policies on education, training, employment and benefits and to develop a coherent and coordinated policy framework.

figure 43
MALCOLM'S STORY

Malcolm is about to move into a flat at the age of 18. He is currently living with his foster mother in an isolated location and will be moving on to an estate in a large village nearby. However, gaining the flat has not been an easy process. Having registered on the waiting list he had to wait for a year to qualify, as he was not originally from the area. There was no choice for Malcolm in the accommodation offered to him. The flat is in a hard to let area which has a poor reputation in the locality. This was a problem for him, as initially he did not feel safe or secure about moving on to the estate. He feels better about this now that he has got to know some of the people who live in the area.

After some initial problems, Malcolm received a Social Services Grant in order to buy furniture for his flat. He has not moved this in yet as the Housing Department are undertaking some repairs to the property and he is concerned that it may be stolen if he is not resident there.

He feels let down by the Housing Authority who persuaded him to sign a tenancy agreement prior to the repairs being carried out, as he has been unable to move in until they are finished, although he is still liable for rent. He considers that this was not properly explained to him.

He has also had a great deal of difficulty receiving Income Support prior to moving from his foster home. His claim has been refused twice due to a need for extra information. He has received good support from a leaving care worker who has helped him with an appeal. Malcolm feels that information has been slow in coming from the relevant agencies. He also feels that the Benefits Agency are discriminating against him because of his background.

(Malcolm's story provided by the Wales Youth Agency)

FAMILY SUPPORT

Family conflict is one of the main triggers to homelessness although, as demonstrated, broader economic and social forces often create or exacerbate these relationship problems and can also make it difficult for young people to find suitable accommodation away from home.

Whatever the underlying causes, however, any preventative strategy should acknowledge the central role that family relations play and include initiatives that will ease family tensions and reduce the likelihood of young people leaving home in a hasty, unplanned way.

There should be a system of positive support and incentives for families to let their children stay at home for longer and overcome relationship problems. In spite of the Government's commitment to the family and its desire to see young people stay at home for longer, the benefit system is, in fact, pushing many young people out of their family homes. The inquiry believes that there should be a review of the ways in which Income Support, Child Benefit, Housing Benefit and the tax system together affect the ability of families to support young people.

Family crisis and mediation services, which offer counselling and mediation to families in conflict, can be an effective way of averting homelessness (see figure 44). However, some young people will have been neglected and abused by their families and so it is essential that family services do not place undue pressure on a young person to remain in or return to the family home.

The right of a young person to confidentiality should also be guaranteed. If possible, such schemes should offer respite accommodation to young people so that problems and solutions can be worked through free of cumulative family tensions.

Young people should be encouraged and helped to keep in touch with their families even if they are unlikely to return home in the immediate future. Pride or fear of rejection often prevents a young homeless person from getting in touch with their parents, and yet once a young person has left the family home it is common for the relationship with his/her parents to improve. By maintaining contact with his/her family a young person is also more likely to receive support while living independently and to feel able to return home at a later date.

figure 44
FAMILY MEDIATION SERVICES

The Home & Away Project, Lambeth

This project was established in 1991 with the aim of preventing youth homelessness by assisting families in conflict where there is a risk that a young person might leave home in an unplanned way. Services are also provided to address the needs of vulnerable young people who are already homeless or living on their own and in need of help and support.

The project works with 13 to 21-year olds in Lambeth, a borough which has a large number of young people who approach central London agencies as homeless. A Family Crisis Service provides a rapid response to families in crisis or where a young person has already left home. A team of four social workers provide a short-term, intensive service for families and young people using solution focused therapy in family or individual sessions. Latest project statistics for 1995 show that 48% of clients were in crisis in their family homes and 52% had already left home.

Following the involvement of the project, 54% of families resolved their crisis and the young person remained at home, while 38% of 13 to 15-year old 'runaways' and 16% of older young homeless people returned home. The great majority of those unable to return home were found other safe accommodation.

The project also has an advice centre which provides advice on housing and benefits and can refer young people on to the crisis service or hostel accommodation. The Advice Centre also provides support to young people moving into permanent accommodation. The project has emergency accommodation which allows for a period of respite while work continues with a young person and their family, and also runs a supported lodgings scheme, a shared house and rent in advance scheme.

St Basil's Family Mediation Project, Birmingham

St Basil's Centre is one of the largest voluntary agencies in Birmingham, each year providing advice, support and accommodation to approximately 1,800 young people. The Centre is involved in a three year pilot family mediation project, which is supported by Birmingham Social Services Department, The Prince's Trust and Charity Projects.

The project involves the development of a model of working with young people and their family and friendship networks which complements the young person centred approach of St Basil's. Young people are helped to explore the relationships they have with their families and friends, usually with a view to re-establishing or increasing contact and reducing conflict.

First of all, with the help of a project worker, a young person decides on a plan of action for how they would like their relationships to develop with family members and other people who are important to them. The way in which contact is made with family members and others depends on circumstances and how a young person wants to proceed. Sometimes, a meeting of all those involved is held, but experience has shown that a more gradual approach is generally most effective. Contact is first of all made with a key member of the young person's family or network, and further contacts usually develop from this.

Since the project started in November 1994 a total of 58 referrals have been received. Almost half of these young people decided not to pursue mediation or moved away. This reflects the transient nature of youth homelessness and the difficulties of resettling into the community. Of those who did proceed, the great majority made contact with their family and consequently relationships within their network improved significantly. In over half the cases the young person was able to return home as a consequence of mediation. Even where a young person is unable to return home the project brings many other benefits. If relationships with family members and other key people improve, a young person is more likely to receive support while living away from home. The project worker can continue to be a point of contact.

Prevention

RECOMMENDATIONS

1 Education

1.1 Local education and housing authorities should liaise to establish an education programme about leaving home, housing options and life/communication skills. Wherever possible, other organisations, such as local voluntary groups, should be involved in the development and delivery of the programme. This should then be introduced to all secondary school and youth work curricula.

1.2 At the age of 14 or 15, each pupil should be provided with an information pack on leaving home, housing and homelessness.

1.3 The Department for Education should encourage all education authorities to introduce education programmes about leaving home, housing/homelessness and life skills in their schools. In consultation with young people and other relevant professionals, they should produce a resource pack which could be used/adapted locally.

1.4 Peer-led initiatives should be facilitated wherever possible.

2 Advice

2.1 There should be comprehensive and accessible advice and information services for young people.

2.2 Local statutory and voluntary agencies should jointly develop a local advice and information service for young people to meet local needs and circumstances. This might include: a dedicated advice centre; information packs and leaflets for young people; out-reach advice and support services; and advocacy services for young people.

3 Preparation and support for young people leaving care

3.1 Social services departments should ensure that all care leavers are adequately prepared and supported when they leave care and that each young person has a care plan. As far as possible, young people should be involved in the development of their care plans.

3.2 In line with the Children Act 1989, and associated guidance and regulations, housing departments and social services departments should cooperate in planning and delivering suitable housing for young people who are, or will be, leaving care. Where appropriate, voluntary agencies should also be fully involved in the provision of housing and support.

3.3 Social services departments should ensure that preparation for leaving care starts early and includes personal and life/communication skills training. Consideration should be given to the establishment of intermediate 'preparation for adulthood' accommodation, although this type of accommodation should not be a compulsory part of the leaving care process.

3.4 Social services departments and local voluntary agencies should set up befriending schemes to provide care-leavers with on-going support, guidance and friendship.

3.5 Social services departments should allow care-leavers, up to the age of 25 years, to return to a suitable care environment when they are in difficulty and in need of additional support.

3.6 Social services departments should give priority to the need for young people to maintain continuity of relationships with social workers, carers and other important people in their lives.

3.7 Social services departments should encourage and support young people in repairing and maintaining links with their families.

3.8 Social services departments should ensure that young people have the finances to maintain housing, training, education and contacts with their families.

4 Young people leaving other institutions

4.1 Statutory and voluntary agencies should ensure that young people leaving other institutions such as prison, hospital or residential care are adequately prepared and supported.

5 Increasing housing opportunities

5.1 Local statutory and voluntary agencies should work in partnership with the private rented sector to increase access for young people to privately rented accommodation and to improve conditions within the sector.

5.2 Wherever possible young people should not be placed in bed and breakfast and poor quality privately rented accommodation, especially if they are vulnerable.

5.3 Local authorities, housing associations and voluntary groups should review their waiting list and allocations policies to ensure that there are no unnecessary access hurdles for young people.

5.4 Local authorities, housing associations and voluntary groups should consider providing some accommodation on a shared basis.

5.5 Local authorities, housing associations and voluntary groups should provide some housing on a furnished or semi-furnished basis; and should assist tenants in unfurnished accommodation to acquire essential items by, for example, setting up a furniture store.

5.6 Local authorities and housing associations should consider converting low demand accommodation, such as high rise and sheltered schemes, for use by young single people.

5.7 Medium to large sized employers should provide employees with grants or loans to help them move and secure suitable accommodation.

6 Increasing educational, training and employment opportunities

6.1 The Government should introduce a comprehensive strategy for tackling unemployment amongst young people.

6.2 There should be further investigation of the potential for non-market work and self-help projects to develop the skills and employment opportunities of young people.

6.3 The Government should ensure that young people who need it have access to intensive pre-vocational training

7 A benefit safety net

7.1 The Government should restore Income Support to 16/17-year olds who are registered for Youth Training and actively seeking work and pay the same level of benefit to 18 to 24-year olds as to those who are 25+ years of age.

7.2 - 7.8 Until benefits are restored to 16 to 24-year olds there should, in the short term, be a number of changes to benefit entitlement to protect those young people in most in need, as follows:

- 7.2 16/17-year olds should be paid benefit at the same rate as for 18 to 24-year olds.
- 7.3 Young people are currently entitled to Income Support during the Child Benefit extension period (usually for about 3 months after leaving school) if they have a good reason for not living at home. As long as they remain on the Youth Training Register and are seeking work, this period should be extended to their 18th birthday.
- 7.4 There should be a right to appeal against decisions regarding severe hardship payments.
- 7.5 Young people undertaking further education in order to further their prospects of employment should receive a subsistence allowance either in the form of a grant or Income Support.
- 7.6 The disregards that apply to earnings should also apply to Youth Training Allowances.
- 7.7 Assessments of whether a young person had good cause to leave employment or training should be made quickly and a young person should not lose benefit while the assessment is being made.
- 7.8 The 16 hour rule, which means that a young person who is on an educational course involving more than 16 hours a week is disqualified from benefit, should either be abolished or revised, to extend the permissible study hours.

7.9 There should a coherent and coordinated policy on education, training, employment and benefit for young people.

8 Family Support

8.1 Family mediation services should be established to: provide support and respite to young people and their families; help prevent homelessness; and help families renew and maintain contacts once young people have left home.

8.2 There should be a review of the ways in which the benefit and tax systems affect the ability of families to support young people. There should be financial incentives for families to continue to accommodate and support their children.

Responding to homelessness

No matter how comprehensive a preventative strategy is, there will inevitably be cases where homelessness cannot be averted. It is therefore essential that there are arrangements in place to help young people who find themselves in the situation of having nowhere to go.

It is important that the needs of young homeless people are assessed as quickly as possible and on an individual basis. As we have seen, young homeless people are not an homogenous group but like the rest of the population have different characteristics, needs and preferences which may change over time.

The great majority of young homeless people need only decent quality accommodation and the sort of practical help that a supportive family and friends would ordinarily provide - for example, help with furnishings and advice on running a home. Once established in their new home, these young people would not usually require very much home-related support, although many would still benefit from schemes which provide social contacts and help to secure training and employment.

There is, however, a small but growing minority of young homeless people who have multiple problems and needs and require much more support, extending in some cases to treatment and rehabilitation. For example, some young people need psychiatric counselling, treatment for drug and/or alcohol addiction and intensive support and on-going aftercare to enable them to live independently. Sarah's story, in figure 45 shows that some young people need support over many years.

In some cases, this specialised and intensive support is best provided in a hostel setting, at least during the early days. Evidence strongly suggests that if a young person's needs are not assessed and the accommodation and support that are provided are inappropriate in some way, there is much more likely to be a problematic transition to independence.

The ways in which agencies should respond when young people become homeless are described under the following headings:-

i) Assessing needs
ii) Strengthening the safety nets
iii) Providing accommodation, support and care

figure 45

SARAH'S STORY

Sarah is 16 years old and has suffered many years of sexual abuse by members of her family. Her family wouldn't listen to her cries for help, and refused to believe her when she spoke out about the abuse. She began to mutilate herself and turned to heavy drinking. Following a suicide attempt, she decided to leave home and enter foster care.

The foster placement did not work out. She felt lonely and depressed - her family did not want to know her. Things deteriorated when an elderly neighbour began to expose himself to her. Her foster mother was 65 and Sarah felt she couldn't talk to her as she wouldn't understand. Again she tried to kill herself, again she was saved. This time, though, she was admitted to a mental hospital. During this period she desperately wanted her family and longed to be happy and normal.

On being discharged from hospital Sarah went back home seeking the love and affection she urgently wanted. However, things did not work out and Sarah once again started to mutilate herself. Things improved slightly when she got a job in a nursing home and enrolled on a college course. She soon made a new group of friends, and between work and study she spent little time at home - keeping busy was her only way of surviving. At times she didn't even go home, she slept on park benches or stayed with friends. She had numerous short-term relationships but found herself being re-abused by the men she was involved with. She was raped by one and attempted suicide shortly afterwards. She was admitted to a mental hospital where she spent 2 months. Whilst in hospital, she continued to cut herself and take overdoses. The staff lost patience with Sarah and threatened to discharge her if she did not stop hurting herself.

Sarah was then placed with foster parents and once again started to have counselling sessions. However, relations with the foster mother were not good, and Sarah found it difficult to talk about her past with the counsellor. She met a man she cared about and became pregnant. Although her boyfriend let her down, Sarah decided to have the baby.

She stopped mutilating her body, left foster care and moved into a house. Her relationship with her family improved and by the time her baby was born Sarah and her family had become friends. Sarah continues to have counselling.

Story provided by the Wales Youth Agency.

ASSESSING NEEDS

We have seen that confusion over the respective responsibilities of different statutory authorities can result in young homeless people falling through the welfare safety nets that have been provided to protect them.

This can be a particular problem for young people with multiple problems and needs which require the involvement of several different agencies. It is essential that local authorities take the lead in agreeing a framework and procedures for receiving, assessing and assisting young homeless people. This framework should cover:

1. referral criteria and procedures;
2. assessment and interpretations of vulnerability;
3. fast track assessments in emergencies;
4. agencies' roles in providing advice, assistance and support;
5. related inter-agency cooperation.

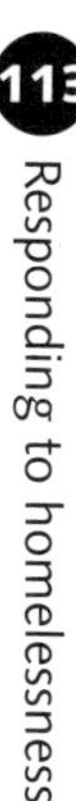

Assessment procedures should aim to:

- build on the young person's main contact with the service network, by using a key contact and bringing in expertise on an as needed basis;
- minimise the extent to which a young person is moved on to other services;
- avoid the situation where a young person with multiple problems falls through the service net.

There needs to be full and early communication on individual cases. At present contacts between agencies tend to be crisis led and come too late in the day. For example, a social services department will contact a housing authority when a young person is on the point of leaving care and a housing organisation might contact a social services department for assistance when they experience management difficulties with a young vulnerable tenant.

In an environment of limited resources, disputes over the relative contributions of housing and care have become commonplace and it is understandable that unexpected requests for assistance are often greeted with resentment. Early contact and discussion between agencies, as part of a pre-agreed referral and assessment framework, could do much to foster cooperation and overcome uncertainties about contributions.

Any framework should include liaison with potential sources of referrals such as prisons, hospitals and care homes. Some young people experience a revolving door of homelessness, offending, custody, homelessness and so on. For example, over half of ex-offenders are under 20-years of age and have multiple personal problems.[21]

Agencies need to break this cycle by making early contact with young people in institutional care and, if necessary, helping them when they leave. Sufficient notice must be given of young vulnerable people being discharged into the community.

There are a number of reasons for the current lack of forward planning -including: poor communication; different authorities have different geographical catchment areas; insufficient attention being paid to those who are considered ineligible under the Children Act, homelessness or community care legislation, and often there is simply insufficient move-on accommodation.

In the case of people discharged from hospital or special units, the pressure on beds and the need for a rapid through-put of patients, often means that little notice of discharge is given.

Advance planning is needed on a number of different levels. Projections of the number of people likely to leave institutions, hostels and special schemes over the next 3 years or so need to be drawn up. These should then be fed into the assessments of overall needs described in the section on Local Strategies on page 127. There should in addition be early warning systems at the operational level.

Housing organisations need notice of the number of people in the year ahead who will be discharged or moved on and who will be in housing need. They also need sufficient warning of when and what type of accommodation will be required by each person. This advance warning system should operate even if an applicant does not qualify for a community-care assessment, since it is possible that they will still need and be eligible for rehousing.

Arrangements should also recognise that young people who are homeless do not always seek help for their homelessness. Initial contact with agencies may be in connection with another problem such as drug misuse or offending. Staff in a variety of different statutory, voluntary and community agencies should be trained to recognise and respond to signs that a young person may be homeless or about to become homeless and when they might be vulnerable.

Certain situations and characteristics should be recognised triggers for further assessment and action. Young people may be escaping from abusive situations and be suspicious of adults, confused or distressed and so it is essential that interviews are sensitively conducted and that mediation does not place a young person at risk.

An information pack and training on how to respond to young people who are or might become homeless should be made available to all front-line staff including benefit officers, GPs, health care workers, accident and emergency staff, careers and training officers, housing officers and social services staff. Joint training and workshops can be a particularly effective way of raising the awareness of service providers to the issue of youth homelessness.

Authorities should seek to agree definitions and the ways in which eligibility will be assessed. Reaching agreement will not always be easy but the changes to statutory definitions and the rights of young homeless people being recommended should reduce the potential for conflict - see *Strengthening the Safety Nets* on page 116.

Housing organisations should lobby for young homeless people to be assessed under the Children Act or community care legislation as there is a strong likelihood of vulnerability and this in itself justifies a referral for assessment.

Statutory authorities also need to appreciate that vulnerable young people often have multiple or non specific problems such as behavioural problems. These young people, whilst not easily assimilated into community care or Children Act priority categories, are often in need of care and support.

It is vital to establish the eligibility of young homeless people to care and support under the Children Act and community care legislation as research has shown that it is difficult to secure these for tenants or applicants if they fall outside the statutory framework.[22] Similarly, care providers need to understand how assessments for housing are undertaken as the eligibility of vulnerable applicants could depend as much on a guarantee that necessary care and support will be provided as on evidence of housing need. Housing authorities appear to be increasingly reluctant to rehouse young vulnerable people if they believe that the support and care they need will not be forthcoming and management problems are likely to result.

In turn, however, housing providers should review their own eligibility criteria in the light of the assessment criteria of caring agencies. For example, if a young person has been found to be eligible under the Children Act or community care legislation, housing providers should consider carefully whether it really is necessary to undertake a further needs assessment. It may be more productive to focus their efforts on jointly developing appropriate housing and care packages.

In arriving at joint assessments of housing and care needs it is essential that young people's own views and preferences are taken into account. This is important even if there is little prospect, in the short term, of these preferences being realised. If recorded assessments are based solely on current provision, and what an applicant is likely to get rather than what he or she wants, there will be no data to support any future improvements to provision. However, assessments must also record what can be realistically secured within a reasonable period of time.

Agreements between different agencies on referrals and assessments should minimise inter-agency wrangling over individual cases and result in fewer young homeless people falling through the safety nets. The Children Act has undoubtedly improved cooperation and coordination between different agencies. However, it is important that these agreements are reasonably formal - possibly drawn up as contracts - since more informal arrangements are likely to break down when budgets are under pressure.(see *Local Strategies* on page 127)

STRENGTHENING THE SAFETY NETS

Although the Children Act, homelessness and community care legislation provide scope for local authorities to respond positively and creatively to the needs of homeless young people, they leave much to the discretion of local authorities.[23] **Local authorities have considerable latitude in how they define 'vulnerability', 'in need' and even 'homelessness', and there is firm evidence that some authorities are choosing to ignore or minimise their legal duties towards young people.**[24]

There are also few rights of appeal which means that young people who are refused assistance have no or little legal recourse and local authorities are rarely penalized for getting it wrong. **The rights of young, vulnerable homeless people to the housing and care they require should be more clearly stated in law including an accessible and speedy system for appeals and more effective remedies against authorities who do not fulfill their duties.**

The Government should revise the priority need categories included in Part III of the Housing Act 1985 (a new housing bill was passing through Parliament when this report went to press) to include all young people leaving care and all young people under the age of 18. There should also be a right of appeal and remedies against authorities who do not meet their duties under the Children Act 1989.

PROVIDING ACCOMMODATION, SUPPORT AND CARE

A RANGE OF DIFFERENT ACCOMMODATION TYPES

It is essential that there is a range of accommodation types. Young homeless people have different needs, they need the chance to move on at their own pace and it is important that accommodation is available immediately in an emergency. The range should include emergency accommodation, medium term and long term accommodation with different levels of support. St Basil's, Birmingham (Figure 46) is a good example of a project with a comprehensive and flexible range of services and good links with other agencies and sectors.

figure 46

PROVIDING A RANGE OF ACCOMMODATION SERVICES TO YOUNG HOMELESS PEOPLE

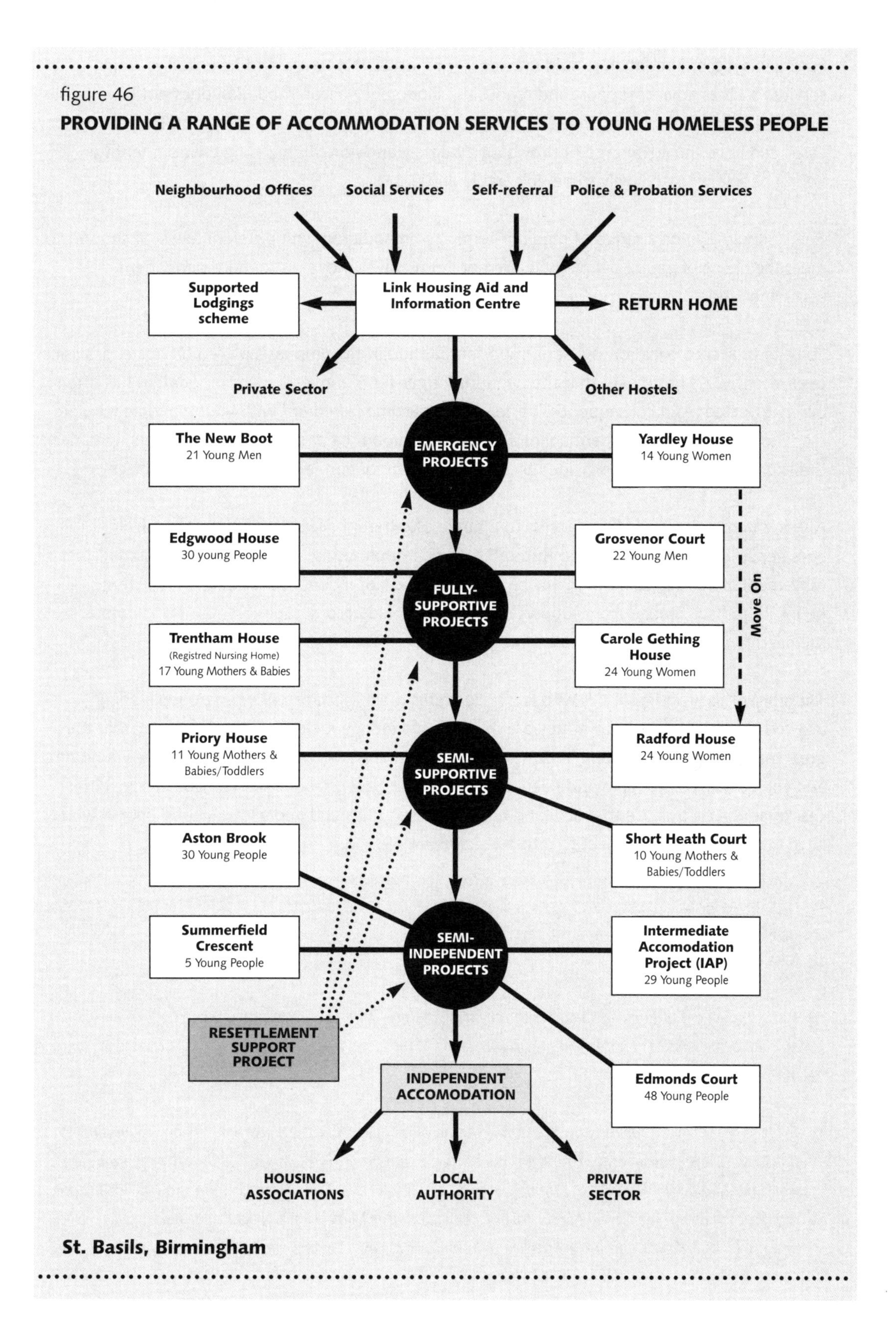

St. Basils, Birmingham

Emergency accommodation should provide a safe, accessible haven and be linked to other services such as advice, support and rehousing. Emergency accommodation does not have to be provided in a hostel type setting. Some supported lodging schemes are geared to take emergency cases and have the advantage of providing a homely and non-stigmatizing environment for young people who are likely to be vulnerable and upset.

There should also be a range of medium-term accommodation with different levels of support to meet the needs of young people who are not yet ready to move on to more permanent accommodation.

Long-term accommodation is just as important, although the emphasis placed on hostel provision over recent years has meant that the need for longer-term, move-on accommodation has often been neglected. As a consequence, hostels often become 'silted up' with young people who are ready to move on to more permanent accommodation but cannot do so, whilst others, who need the extra support and care provided by hostel accommodation, are unable to find a place.

Although projects should have access to a range of different accommodation types, from emergency/crisis accommodation through to long-term housing, it should not be assumed that all movement along this continuum will be in the direction of independent living. Some young people who have moved from supported to unsupported accommodation may, for example, feel the need to return temporarily to a more protected environment.

The story of Sally, in figure 47, who is 23, illustrates the importance of young people being allowed several chances before they are ready to live independently. We saw in Part 1 that the great majority of young people return to the family at least once before they finally leave home, and young homeless people also need access to a safe haven. The Broad Horizons project in Clackmannan District, Central Scotland has recognised this need and allows young people who have been through the project to return - see figure 49.

figure 47
SALLY'S STORY

I was thrown out of home at 15 and with it being Christmas Day, this emphasized my feelings of desolation and not being wanted. Thank God my brother knew of the YMCA. A haven away from the emotional abuse of home.

I stayed at the YMCA for three years. Although I did move out to share a house with my boyfriend during this time - I think it was my yearning for independence and proof that I was an adult - anyway that didn't work out! So back to the YMCA. I think that was essential for me. The support if I did want to venture out into my own independence but the security of knowing that if I mucked up I could come back to the YMCA and not be regarded as a failure - I needed to learn from my own lessons and mistakes - no one else's would

have an effect on me. I carried on with this pattern for several years - I had to have the time to discover myself, my strengths and weaknesses and I was given that time by my social workers to find my own way and independence.

I see more of my Dad and Step-mum now and things are a lot easier and I suppose you can say that time does heal!! I'm now working and have definite plans for my future, I'm saving hard to spend some time doing voluntary work in the YMCA in West Africa. This has been my own decision and it has given me something to aim for and a real purpose.
Sally aged 23

There is a need for more high care accommodation for very vulnerable young people. However, there is very little information available on the most effective ways of providing such services which means that there is a very real danger of expensive mistakes being made. The inquiry believes that this area of need and the most appropriate responses requires further research and that guidance should be subsequently issued to housing and care providers.

There is a wide range of different models for providing housing and care to young people, from shared and self-contained supported housing, hostels, supported lodgings to support in mainstream tenancies. There is no ideal type or package of provision. However, it is must be based upon the assessed needs of young people and these needs must be evaluated over time.

Provision should not be determined solely by funding sources and mechanisms or slavishly follow standard or fashionable models of provision. It is also important that, wherever possible, young people are closely involved in the development and running of the services they use. The great majority want to be actively involved in shaping their future and participation helps to build self-reliance and adult life skills.

figure 48
A COMPREHENSIVE SERVICE TO HOMELESS YOUNG PEOPLE

The Young Homeless Project, Warwickshire
This project, established in 1993, now includes a housing support and advice centre, which supports and advises young people on housing, welfare benefits and related issues. It includes: a Nightstop scheme, which provides emergency accommodation for young people faced with rough sleeping; a supported accommodation project which provides shared and individual housing for young people who wish to live independently but also need support to take the first step after leaving home; a private sector initiative which operates a register of rented accommodation in the private sector and rent deposit vouchers and rent in advance payments; a supported lodgings scheme which offers lodging with various levels of support to those young people who have no experience of living on their own. During 1995/6, the project saw 331 young people and found accommodation for 123.

Time Stop, Peterborough YMCA

Established in 1992, Time Stop is both a hostel and a drop-in centre for young people. The project is run by Peterborough YMCA but closely involves a range of different statutory and voluntary agencies. It provides a wide range of different services on the grounds that "the provision of a key to a dwelling only partially addresses the issue surrounding youth homelessness". The Centre offers counselling services, a drop-in centre, emergency and short-term accommodation (for up to 10 days and 3 months), medium term housing for 138 young people, proactive preventative work, reconciliation services and re-settlement work. During 1995, almost 4,000 young people used the drop-in centre, more than 900 received counselling, 168 were accommodated by the project and over 150 young people were helped to find alternative accommodation.

figure 49

THE CHANCE TO RETURN TO A SUPPORTED ENVIRONMENT

Broad Horizons, Clackmannshire - Re-referral Scheme

Broad Horizons is a medium stay supported accommodation project for 16 to 24 year old vulnerable single homeless people in Clackmannan district, Central Scotland. In 1994 the NCH Action for Children Project introduced a policy of allowing young people to refer themselves to the project, having left of their own free will or having been asked to leave for a particular reason.

The decision was taken to allow re-referrals because it became clear that some young people need several experiences of the project before they have matured to a level where they are able and willing to make a commitment to independent living. During 1995/96, 23 of the total of 46 young people were re-referrals within the year, although some had been resident within the Project during previous years. 4 of the 23 who re-referred during 1995/96 stayed more than once during the year.

ON-GOING AND COMPREHENSIVE SUPPORT

The need for help and support will not always fall away once a young person has been given a key to the door of longer-term accommodation. Many young people will need help moving and settling into their new home, and some will require support on a longer term basis.

It is, therefore, important that support is available on a 'floating' or flexible basis to young people living in a range of different housing situations and is not only tied to hostel accommodation. Another advantage of floating support schemes is that the level and type of support can be relatively easily adjusted in line with a young person's changing needs.

Kevin's story, below, shows the importance of getting the level of support right. Supported lodgings gave him too little independence and in a flat of his own he felt lonely and isolated, but shared accommodation with support from visiting project workers has provided the right combination.

figure 50
KEVIN'S STORY

I went home one night and the door was locked. My dad told me, you don't live here anymore . I was 16 years old and homeless. I was afraid and not sure what to do. A friend's dad said I should try the YMCA, which I did. Eventually after quite a bit of social services red tape I came to live at the Norwich YMCA.

I was still at school when I moved to the YMCA. My family did not try to contact me. I tried and so did my social worker to contact my family, but they were not interested. I still do not understand, even today why all the problems happened between me and my family. Eventually I went to the staff and said I wanted to move out.

Social Services placed me in supported lodgings, but the landlady wanted to mother me too much, so I moved out to a flat that Social Services helped me find, but I wasn't happy and felt very lonely. I went to the advice centre for young people in Norwich and I got the address of the place where I am now. It's ideal and I'm really happy. I share a large house with four other people and project workers come and visit, so its semi-independent.

I'm much more settled and life is beginning to go really well. I now have two part- time jobs - one at the YMCA where I used to live and I also work part-time at Norwich Union. I'm much happier than I have been in ages.
Kevin, aged 17 years.

In Part 1 we saw that many young homeless people have more than just a housing problem - for example, the great majority are unemployed, on low incomes, have poor health and no or little family support. The provision of housing is often, therefore, only part of the solution. A home but no job, money, family support or local friends does not provide a very promising foundation for adulthood. Any lasting solution to youth homelessness requires an holistic approach which can meet a range of different needs. These wider types of support are not just the 'icing on the cake', but have a very significant impact on whether or not rehousing will be successful.

Newcastle City Council's experience of rehousing 16/17-year olds demonstrates the critical importance of on-going support. The Council has been rehousing 16/17-year olds since 1984, and in 1994 decided with First Move, a joint council and voluntary sector team who provide support to young people, to monitor a cohort of 100 homeless 16/17-year olds.[25] Around a half of the cohort had been rehoused by the end of the first year but a disturbingly high proportion reported feeling lonely, isolated and depressed.

On a number of indicators, the group were worse off following rehousing than before. On the whole they were receiving very little formal or informal support - for example, none of the cohort had been assessed by the social services department under Children Act provisions. One surprising interim finding is that young women who have had babies following rehousing experienced an improvement in their health and general outlook. The study, which will continue for several years, at this stage concludes:

Our interim finding is that rehousing makes some problems worse, and that there is no prospect of help from anyone except friends and family. The fact that family relations seem to improve is important but unlikely to compensate for all the needs of the group. Many of the group are from care, and many have been abused at home. Surviving is a testament to the resilience of the group.[25]

The support provided to young people should cover a range of different needs, including: health issues (figure 51); practicalities related to setting up and managing their own home including financial and benefit advice (figure 52); and help to secure education, training or employment. In some cases it will be necessary to arrange for specialist support - for example, to help a young person overcome a drug or alcohol dependency problem (figure 53).

figure 51
SUPPORT WITH HEALTH ISSUES

Hertfordshire Health Action Scheme

Hertfordshire Health Authority and County Council have jointly funded a Health and Homelessness Development Worker to work with homeless people, initially for a period of 12 months.

By providing better health information to homeless people and improving access to GPs and other health services, it is hoped that the number of unplanned pregnancies and health problems amongst homeless people will be reduced. The information collected by the health worker will also be used in the development of appropriate services for homeless people with mental health problems.

The need for a dedicated health worker was highlighted by the results of a health survey of homeless people undertaken in 1994. Half of those surveyed said they were suffering from depression, a third had sex all or most of the time without a condom and a third of those who had tried to see a doctor had experienced problems. Local agencies have also reported increasing numbers of young homeless people with mental health problems.

figure 52
SUPPORT WITH MOVING INTO NEW ACCOMMODATION

Cardiff Move-on Ltd.

This is a floating support scheme, established to increase the number of permanent council and housing association lettings that are made available to young people living in temporary or voluntary sector accommodation. Peripatetic support is provided on a flexible, as required basis to ensure that young people successfully maintain their tenancies. The scheme operates on a referral basis and involves assessment of the housing and support needs of referrals and the preparation of support packages that will help young people through the physical move and the settling down period. Around a third of their clients are under 25 years old.

Cardiff Move-on Ltd is part of Cardiff's Single Homelessness Strategy and relies heavily on the cooperation and participation of the whole of the voluntary sector as well as Cardiff County Council and local housing associations

figure 53
SUPPORT FOR SUBSTANCE MISUSERS

Coventry and Warwickshire Substance Misusers' Initiative
This initiative provides drug misusers with good quality housing association properties and intensive, personalized support to help them overcome their problems.

The scheme, which is run by Warwickshire probation service with Rugby NHS and Jephson Homes and Orbit Housing Associations, is based on the principle that people need good quality stable accommodation before they can begin to tackle their problems.

Accommodation is let on a 6 month probationary basis with the requirement that tenants cooperate with their support workers. Two support workers provide intensive support to 10 clients. The scheme has so far been very successful - 8 of the first 10 clients have been recommended for permanent tenancies and are progressing well.

The scheme which is funded by the Probation Service and a Special Needs Housing Management Allowance from the Housing Corporation, has won £2m from the Government's single regeneration budget which will provide six years further funding and another 20 flats.

A number of studies, including the Newcastle City Council cohort study mentioned earlier, have found that isolation and loneliness are often major problems for young homeless people, especially once they have been rehoused. Having your own flat may be safer, healthier and more comfortable than living on the streets or in a crowded hostel but it is not usually as sociable. Young people who are sleeping rough often say that the most positive aspect of the experience is the strong bonds that develop between young people in the same position.

Young people, especially those without family support, need help to build up social and support networks, before the loneliness of living alone becomes too much for them and they fall into homelessness again. Wherever possible, young people should be given the option of living in shared housing or accommodation with some communal areas, and agencies should consider establishing befriending schemes, drop-in centres and youth clubs (figure 54).
It is also important that young people are encouraged to renew or maintain contacts with their families. We have seen earlier in this chapter how, if given the chance, family relationships often improve once a young person has left home and thereafter the family can become an important source of support.

There are a number of young people who seem to self-destruct. Their drug use results in eviction or self-harm or damage to property. Disputes with neighbours or their peer group leads to criminal damage or violence, all of which returns the person back to being homeless. However, how reasonable is it to place a young person in a run down bedsit or flat with little money and expect them to function as a responsible person? In many cases young people will only achieve stability in their lives with outreach support - support that is client led, practical and takes account of personal circumstances and skills.

St Anne's, Leeds

figure 54

SOCIAL OPPORTUNITIES AND SUPPORT

ByPass - Bolton's Advice and Drop-in Centre for Young People

The Bypass advice and drop-in centre was opened in March 1993 in a shop in the heart of Bolton town centre. The centre, which is for 16 to 25 year olds, provides advice and information, an advocacy service (developed by Save the Children and Bolton Social Services), an accommodation project and opportunities for young people to meet each other informally for a coffee and a chat.

There is a coffee bar, créche, a clothing store which offers clothes for sale and for swapping, a laundry, shower and clean-up facilities and a food co-op which provides food at below market prices. Young people are actively involved in the running of the centre and belong to a planning group which discusses issues that affect the centre and young people more generally.

Funding for the centre comes from a variety of sources. In 1994/95 grants were received from Bolton Social Services, Bolton Housing Department, Bolton Youth Service, The Department of Health, the local Health Authority and Save the Children.

Artswork Young People at Risk Project

Artswork is a national youth arts organisation which specialises in working with young people between the ages of 14 and 19 years who would otherwise miss out on arts opportunities.
A new national programme Young People at Risk Project (YPAR), funded by the BBC Children in Need Appeal, works specifically with young people at risk including homeless people. The project uses arts to help young people build confidence, face problems and come up with solutions. YPAR has established four pilot projects as part of the initiative, including a theatre project in Cumbria.

The Cumbria project has involved 40 young people writing, designing and acting a theatre piece on the subject of housing and related issues for young people in Cumbria. Their performance was successfully toured in June and July 1996 at youth and community centres and professional venues.

Responding to Homelessness

RECOMMENDATIONS

1 Assessing needs

1.1 Local authorities, in conjunction with housing associations and voluntary agencies, should establish a framework and procedures for receiving, assessing and assisting young homeless people so that they are not passed unnecessarily from one agency to another. These agreements are particularly important in respect of vulnerable young people.

1.2 Staff in a wide range of front-line agencies - such as general medical practices, benefit offices, schools, advice agencies - should be made aware of the problems of youth homelessness and advised and trained on how to respond.

2 Strengthening the Safety Nets

2.1 The Government should revise the priority need categories included in the homelessness legislation (presently the Housing Act 1985, Part III - though when this report went to press a new Housing Bill was passing through Parliament) to include all young people leaving care and all 16/17-year olds.

2.2 The Government should introduce a right of appeal and more effective remedies against authorities who do not fulfill their duties under the Children Act 1989.

3 Providing Accommodation, Care and Support

3.1 Statutory and voluntary agencies should ensure that the accommodation and services provided to young people are based on assessments of individual needs. The match between needs and the services provided to each young person should be reviewed at regular intervals.

3.2 The need for high support accommodation for vulnerable young people with multiple needs should be investigated at the local and national level.

3.3 Projects for young people should have access to a range of different accommodation types, including emergency accommodation, medium and longer-term accommodation, with appropriate levels of support.

3.4 Statutory and voluntary agencies should allow young people, who have moved on to longer-term housing, to return to supported accommodation during periods of crisis.

3.5 Statutory and voluntary agencies should continue to provide support on a flexible, as needed basis once young people have moved into longer-term accommodation.

3.6 Statutory and voluntary agencies should recognise that homelessness is only part of the problem for many young people. As well as the more usual housing and support schemes, agencies should establish initiatives that will help young people into education, training and employment, improve the health of young people and encourage the development of social and support networks that will help young people during the transition to independence.

3.7 Statutory and voluntary agencies should actively involve young people in the development and management of the services they receive.

Local strategies

If we really want to change the environment in which agencies are operating so that we can genuinely improve the housing options of young people at a local level, we need to have a plan. We must know what the problem is by listening to young people and those that work with them. We must produce a strategy to tackle the problem and we must combine resources from across agencies to implement the strategy. It sounds easy, but to coordinate activity across such diverse sectors as housing, social services, health, education and employment is a complex task. Somebody must act as a catalyst to galvanize the agencies into action, and to ensure that young people's voices are heard. That 'somebody' may be the local authority or an independent agency, but whoever it is, they need to be properly resourced and they need to start work now.
Jeremy Spafford, Centrepoint

A local strategy provides a framework and a focus for the preventative and remedial initiatives described in Sections 6 and 7. There is an urgent need for greater cooperation and coordination not just at the operational level - for example in the ways in which agencies assess and respond to individual cases of youth homelessness - but also at the strategic level.

A strategic and coordinated approach is needed because of the diversity of the needs of young homeless people and the wide array of different organisations, with varying roles, responsibilities and client groups, who provide services to them. This fragmentation is in large part due to the fact that young people are not usually a priority group for statutory services and so a myriad of small voluntary sector agencies have stepped in to meet the needs that so clearly exist. Whilst the predominance of voluntary agencies has many advantages (for example, they generally have a good understanding of local problems and needs), a patchwork of different agencies and projects can create difficulties if they are not underpinned by a cohesive local strategy.

Without an over-arching plan or strategy there is no guarantee that the most urgent needs of young people are being met. There can be unnecessary and wasteful duplication of services and difficulties for young people in finding their way around the bewildering maze of different organisations.

A review of the sector and organisational issues, undertaken for the inquiry by McKinsey & Company, found that currently available resources are having less than their potential impact because:

i) there is no agreement among the players in the sector on the definition or size of the target group, nor on the segments within the group, and how to deal with them;
ii) initiatives aimed at coordinating a response are still the exception, and their success to date has been limited;
iii) the volatility of the sector itself makes coordinated, focused action difficult and it may be that the system is diverting resources into too many projects which are too small to be sustained.

A summary of the paper by McKinsey & Company, *Collaborating for success: organisational issues facing the youth homelessness sector* is included at Appendix 5.

There is an urgent need for a more strategic and coordinated approach. Existing resources would be used more effectively since services would be better targeted and would more directly match the needs and preferences of young homeless people.

Also, by raising the profile of the issue, through demonstrating that needs have been properly assessed and that priorities are the result of a comprehensive planning process, agencies should also find it easier to involve other organisations, such as businesses and local charitable trusts to secure new funding.

For example, the Oxfordshire strategic planning initiative described in figure 55, raised £1.8m for young people's projects. There are other rewards for participating organisations, including - a greater sense of direction and purpose and greater cooperation both within and between organisations.

Research by CHAR[26] and the review by McKinsey & Company have found that although there is a growing awareness amongst local agencies of the importance of responding strategically to the problem of youth homelessness, there has been little progress to date. Where strategies and forums on youth homelessness do exist, their impact has largely been confined to improving information sharing between local agencies on the ground.

Local strategies do not appear to have reduced homelessness substantially or to have increased the resources available to homeless people (McKinsey and Company). However, **local strategies do have the potential to make a very real difference to service delivery on the ground.** They can provide a spur to action, a framework for the provision of services and the focus for fund and awareness raising.

We would expect that the resources available to help young homeless people would achieve more impact if the sector was better organised to channel funds according to needs-based local strategies.
McKinsey and Company, 1996.

Those authorities without a strategy tend to view single homeless people as a very low priority and not their responsibility. They tend to have a narrow definition of their role in relation to single people and in the main will only provide advice and assistance.
CHAR, 1996.[26]

Although there is no blueprint for carrying the strategic approach forward, the models for partnership and coordination that presently exist suggest that there are a number of key elements and these are discussed below.

GETTING STARTED

It is critically important that any local strategy on youth homelessness is both comprehensive and consensual. It must involve the majority of relevant local organisations, including statutory and voluntary agencies, housing associations, local businesses, charitable trusts and, of course, young people themselves. Given the fragmentation of the sector and the diverse needs of young people, this means there is potentially a very large number of organisations to involve.

Some areas have very successfully kick-started their strategic initiative by holding a conference on young people and housing and care needs to which a wide array of different organisations were invited.

For example, in October 1995, Hampshire County Council, Portsmouth City Council and Portsmouth Housing Association held a conference entitled 'Why Invest In Young People' to consider a range of issues affecting young people including housing and employment. More than 120 people from over 40 different organisations attended and as a consequence plans to establish youth fora throughout the County and a South East Hampshire Youth Strategy are well advanced.

Once a basic agenda for the initiative has been agreed, it is often more practical for a core group, forum or facilitator to take things forward. For example, in Oxfordshire, Centrepoint's National Development Unit has helped to develop a local strategy on youth homelessness (see figure 55). Since Centrepoint does not own or manage projects in the area it is not competing for resources and is seen to be independent.

The organisation's objectivity and expertise have won the support of local agencies and much has been achieved in the few years since the project started. The Oxfordshire project was established as a pilot for strategic planning on youth homelessness and Centrepoint is already facilitating strategic initiatives in other areas of the country.

Some areas have appointed policy coordinators to work specifically in the area of youth homelessness. For example, the London Borough of Lewisham has a Young Homeless Policy Coordinator, jointly funded by Social Services and the Housing Department, whose brief it is to formulate a joint policy between the two departments and to make recommendations on policies for 16/17-year olds.

Whatever the approach adopted, it is essential that there is formal commitment and support from senior management. If this high level support is not forthcoming, there is a danger that local strategy groups will become talking shops with no power to influence policy and practice.

figure 55

CENTREPOINT OXFORDSHIRE - A REGIONAL STRATEGY ON YOUTH HOMELESSNESS

A project to establish a regional strategy on youth homelessness in Oxfordshire was launched in December 1991. The project was funded by the Department of the Environment and was undertaken by Centrepoint's National Development Unit in close cooperation with local agencies. There were three main strands to the project:-

1. *to produce a report describing provision for young people in housing need across the county and identifying gaps in provision;*
2. *to publish a strategy showing how those gaps could be filled and by whom;*
3. *to work in conjunction with partner agencies to develop policies, schemes and projects recommended in the strategy.*

Following extensive research and consultation, the strategy - Housing Young People in Oxfordshire - was published in 1992. The report identifies 12 key priority areas as follows.

1. *Emergency accommodation.*
2. *Social housing.*
3. *Support.*
4. *Private rented sector.*
5. *Advice, information and drop-in facilities.*
6. *Education - preparation for leaving home.*
7. *Employment.*
8. *Health.*
9. *Inter-agency working.*
10. *Consulting and involving young people.*
11. *Equal opportunities.*
12. *Preparing for the end of the project.*

The strategy also identifies a list of projects for each of the towns of the County which could meet the needs that have been identified. The strategy has also been used as the basis for inter-agency cooperation. Centrepoint has worked closely with local agencies in identifying need and the provision required to meet it and then finding ways of setting this in motion. All developments have been steered and managed by local groups. In practical terms, Centrepoint has offered support in areas such as project design, fund-raising, developing policies and procedures and project management. It has also lobbied within the County to improve policies affecting homeless young people and has raised public awareness about youth homelessness.

With the help of local agencies, the Centrepoint Oxfordshire project has raised £1.8m for young people's projects, developed 90 units of social housing and generated 5 new drop-in/advice centres.

MEASURING NEEDS

Before agencies develop a local strategy to meet the needs of young homeless people in their area, they must undertake research into what is currently provided and what is needed.

In spite of being much more aware of the need to assess general housing needs as part of their strategic function, very few local authorities measure the needs of young people. This is due both to methodological difficulties (see Part 1, Section 1) and to the fact that young people are not deemed a priority compared to other applicants.

Authorities need to recognise that by ignoring the problem of youth homelessness they do not remove it - more young people simply end up on the streets and in poor quality bed and breakfast hotels and squats. And if they continue in these precarious and often dangerous situations for long their problems will multiply and intensify.

Some local authorities fear that they will be unable to cope with the level of need uncovered by a needs assessment. However, it is only by conducting such an assessment that an authority will have a comprehensive picture of the local situation, be able to prioritize needs, and involve other agencies and sectors in meeting them.

There is an urgent need for guidance to local agencies on the ways in which youth homelessness should be defined and measured. The Department of the Environment has accepted that, given the range of different methodologies applied, there is a case for issuing guidance on how local needs assessments should be conducted.[27] It is essential that this guidance covers the issue of youth homelessness. Ideally, needs should be measured on an on-going basis using the day to day management and information systems of local agencies. Commissioned one-off studies can be useful but they are expensive and quickly become dated. The application, assessment, admission and discharge forms of different agencies should include common questions so that they can be aggregated and analysed over time. Information should be collected on:

- age;
- gender;
- ethnic group;
- disability and health;
- sexuality;
- housing circumstances;
- last settled accommodation;
- reason for housing need;
- experiences of local authority care and other institutions;
- accommodation and care needed;
- accommodation and care provided and outcomes;
- other needs, including training, education, employment.

Some of this information may be too sensitive to collect immediately but the intention should be to build up a detailed and accurate picture of young people's circumstances and needs. Any monitoring system needs to take account of both double and under-counting and should be able to separately identify different groups, including: 16/17-year olds; black and ethnic minority young people; and vulnerable/special needs groups such as young offenders and young people leaving care.

Given the diverse circumstances and needs of young homeless people, it is important that any monitoring or one-off research exercise considers a broad range of needs, including health, education, training, employment.

ESTABLISHING A COMPREHENSIVE STRATEGY

It is often assumed that a housing strategy is predominantly about calculating the need for new housing. Although this is important, it should only form part of a comprehensive housing strategy. Any youth homelessness strategy should also review and improve current policies, practices and provision across a range of different services, including the ways in which different agencies work together. The different processes involved in setting up a local strategy on youth homelessness are shown in figure 56.

The process may seem complex and demanding, but it need not be difficult and it offers many rewards. It should be viewed as a series of logical stages, each with its own valuable output. The process itself must involve as many relevant organisations as possible; cover a broad range of different needs and services; and generate a high level of commitment to the objectives of the exercise.

It is also important that the results from the strategic process feed into policies and development programmes, and that provision to young single people is not viewed in isolation from services to other groups.

figure 56

DRAWING UP A COMPREHENSIVE YOUNG PERSONS' HOUSING STRATEGY

1 agree on the strategic planning process

If the strategic planning process is to be effective, it is essential that the agencies involved reach early agreement on the objectives and coverage of the exercise and the process to be followed. The objectives of the exercise, the areas to be covered, the roles and responsibilities of different organisations, the timetable and the resources required must all be clearly stated and realistic.

Ideally the planning process should cover the areas listed below.

- Advisory services.
- Assessment, referral and joint working arrangements.
- Accommodation services including emergency, furnished and temporary accommodation, supported accommodation and residential care facilities, patterns of use and standards in other types of accommodation such as houses in multiple occupation.
- Joint work focused on preventing homelessness. This includes the need for inter-agency agreements on warning procedures, joint case conferences, the role of key working and coordination functions.
- Support provision and joint work arrangements including resettlement and community based support services.
- Links between homelessness and community care.
- Educational, training and employment opportunities.
- Health issues.
- Social and community issues.
- A strategy on monitoring and reviewing youth homelessness trends and issues.
- Gender and minority interests and needs.

2 agree overall aims and values

Without establishing an early, broadly based consensus on some of the most important values and issues (such as the appropriateness of different models of provision for different groups) a planning group is likely to find the later stages of drawing up more detailed programmes problematic.

Different organisational cultures, values and priorities need to be raised and discussed as early as possible so that areas of conflict can be minimized and areas of agreement maximised. Early agreement on shared values and direction can also help to bond a group and give it the enthusiasm and commitment required to see the planning process through. Once this is done it is often more effective to create a core group to carry out detailed work.

3 assessing overall needs

A coordinated, inter-agency assessment of youth homelessness trends should be made. This should recognise that statistics are likely to under-count and that agencies' monitoring systems will vary. The assessment should clarify the aspects of need listed below.

- Applications by 16/17-year olds and 18 to 25-year olds.
- Gender and race patterns.
- Vulnerability issues, including special needs, young people from care and young adult offenders.
- Other needs - including health, education, training, employment.

This assessment should draw on the experience of local authorities and voluntary agencies, for example, in relation to:

- applications;
- admissions;
- discharges, length of stay and evictions;
- accommodation and support services - taking account of standards of provision and gaps in services.

4 review of policies, procedures and resources

A review should be undertaken which would cover the issues listed below.

- The range and appropriateness of services on offer, taking account of the variety of needs and the quality and effectiveness of services.
- The need for consistency of policy and practice on a comprehensive (24 hour) basis so that out of hours and standby services are integrated with other homelessness services.
- The areas in which it might be relevant and feasible to increase joint work between statutory and voluntary agencies.
- Opportunities for resource pooling and resource sharing to enable new initiatives and more effective services.
- Opportunities to make more use of private sector accommodation.
- An assessment of pipe-line provision and of funding that is likely to become available over the plan period.

5 plan of action

The plan should outline the responsibilities and contributions of statutory and voluntary agencies, taking account of local needs, services and resources. It should specify priorities, responsibilities, targets and time-scales for action.

6 monitoring

Monitoring against targets and time-scales is an essential part of the strategic planning process. Working assumptions, objectives and programmes should be closely and continuously monitored and, if necessary, adjustments made to the strategy and plans.

DEVELOPING LINKS WITH OTHER STRATEGIES

In rural areas or smaller communities it may be more practical to address youth homelessness within a more broadly based strategy - for example covering single homelessness, homelessness or special needs. Even if a separate youth homelessness strategy is drawn up it is essential that it dovetails with other local strategies. A plethora of different strategies with overlapping functions and client groups could create unnecessary work and confusion and, as a consequence, the interests of young homeless people could be further marginalised.

SHARING INFORMATION AND GOOD PRACTICE

There should be a comprehensive and up-to-date inter-agency network of information about agencies' policies, procedures and services. The Internet has enormous potential here and yet the inquiry has found no examples of it being used in this way. A shared information facility could also provide up-to-date information on accommodation vacancies in the private and public sectors and also possibly act as a clearing house for accommodation placements.

At the moment a local agency hoping to find accommodation for a young person usually has to ring around several different organisations and/or landlords before a vacancy is found. The internet has already been applied successfully in this way in Australia. In Victoria, for example, the Info Xchange offers public access to up-to-date information on housing, youth and related issues 24 hours a day, seven days a week. It includes a listing of the support services provided by different agencies and a daily updated listing of accommodation vacancies.

The number of different agencies involved with the welfare of young people suggests that establishing a common register of information should be a priority. With a certain amount of local coordination, modern technology offers the possibility of this being easily accessible and up-to-the minute which would open up many operational possibilities.

It is also important that local strategic planning groups learn from the experiences of others. The inquiry recommends that a national data-base is established so that information and experiences can be shared.

figure 57

A STRATEGY FOR YOUNG SINGLE PEOPLE, SOUTH RIBBLE

Following a seminar held by South Ribble Borough Council in April 1993 on the issue of single homelessness, South Ribble KEY Project was established in March 1994 as a two year project to provide advice to young (16-25) single homeless people, to research the housing needs of this group, and to develop a long-term strategy to meet those needs.

KEY is a partnership between a range of agencies, both statutory and voluntary, including South Ribble Borough Council, the local Council for Voluntary Services, Lancashire County Council Youth and Community Service and Social Services Department, local housing associations, the Area Health Authority, Barnardos and the Princes Trust. The project, which has one full-time worker employed by Barnardos, is registered as a charity and is overseen by a board of trustees. The project has the following aims.

1. *To work directly with homeless young people and those at risk of homelessness.*
2. *To produce specific medium and long-term strategies to meet the unmet accommodation and associated needs of young people.*

3. To have available good information about the needs of young homeless people in South Ribble.
4. To support and develop the local network of existing voluntary and statutory agencies in order to coordinate and support their activities.

In its first year of operation, the KEY project was approached by over 250 young people who were homeless or in housing need. It has also undertaken detailed research into the circumstances and needs of young homeless people in South Ribble. In January 1996 the project published a draft strategy document on young single homelessness which was the product of widespread consultation. The strategy document outlines the background to the project and the research findings and discusses the need for a coordinated and joint approach to service provision, including schemes to: improve the advice and information provided to young people; make more use of the private rented sector; improve drug rehabilitation and health services to young people; and provide more emergency and supported accommodation.

Although the strategy document has been produced by KEY, the aim is for all relevant agencies to feel that they 'own' the document and its objectives. A seminar to publicise the document was held in March 1996 and a wide range of agencies are currently feeding back their comments.

Local strategies

RECOMMENDATIONS

1 Local agencies should work together to develop a joint strategy to meet the needs of young homeless people in their area. The strategy should be based on a comprehensive survey of local needs, should involve young people, and should include preventative as well as remedial initiatives.
2 A pilot project should be developed to test the feasibility of using an internet website for local information on facilities and accommodation vacancies for young people.
3 There should be a national data-base on local youth homelessness strategies, so that local groups can share information and learn from the experiences of others.

A national priority

Government must recognise that youth homelessness is a serious and divisive social problem that requires urgent and coordinated action.

Although much can be achieved at the local level to reduce homelessness amongst young people, the problem can only be effectively tackled if it becomes a national policy priority.

youth homelessness is an issue that cuts across legislative and departmental boundaries. **A range of Government departments, including the Department of the Environment, Home Office, the Department of Social Security and the Department of Health, are responsible for policies that affect young people and yet there is very little coordination. The policies of different departments often undermine each other.**

The inquiry is deeply concerned about the effects that high rents and Housing Benefit restrictions are having on the incentives for young people to find accommodation and employment.

We have seen elsewhere in this report that **recent benefit and housing policies have created the perverse situation of young people being financially better off unemployed and on the streets than rehoused and in employment.** This is just one example of Government policies working against rather than in support of each other. Housing policies that increase rents are hindering other Government policies to get young people into employment and benefit rules are preventing young people securing accommodation.

This policy confusion is not just because so many different Government departments are involved in the creation of policies that affect young people. It is also because Government as a whole lacks a unified and positive vision of what it wants for this country's young people.

Different Government departments must work together to draw up a strategic and positive programme of action to help young people into housing and employment. There are a number of examples of inter-departmental initiatives effectively tackling problems that straddle different departmental interests. The Rough Sleepers' Initiative, which has been spearheaded by an inter-departmental working group, is a good example of what can be achieved given the commitment. The inquiry believes that there is a very strong case for establishing a Ministerial Working Party on Youth Issues.

There is no reason to delay these initiatives. We have most of the information we need to be able to move towards a solution and if we delay, the problem will escalate and become more difficult and expensive to put right. Many of the initiatives described in this report would involve no or very little cost and so there can be no defense for continuing to turn a blind eye to the problems of youth homelessness.

A national priority

RECOMMENDATIONS

1. The Government should draw up a coordinated and positive programme of action to tackle the problem of youth homelessness and improve the life chances of young people.
2. A Ministerial Working Party or a Minister with special responsibility for young people, should be responsible for developing the national programme of action.
3. The Department of the Environment should ensure that national housing needs projections include single people who are living with other households.
4. The Department of the Environment should issue guidance to local authorities on needs assessment methods, require regular statistical returns from local authorities on the number of non priority homeless people in their area (including young single people) and regularly publish the results.
5. Further research should be undertaken in the following areas:
   - the growth in the number of very vulnerable young homeless people, including those with mental health and emotional problems, and their housing and care needs;
   - the effectiveness of non-market and self help employment and housing initiatives;
   - a pilot project to establish a local web-site providing information on local services and vacancies for young people;
   - the effects of the October 1996 Housing Benefit changes on young people's access to the private rented sector;
   - the housing problems and needs of lesbians and gay men;
   - the effectiveness of peer-led approaches.

References

BY SECTION

PART 1
SECTION 1

1. A median figure has been calculated from 12 local surveys (submitted as evidence) of the proportion of young people who were sleeping rough when they approached a housing or advice agency.
2. See, for example, The Children Act and Young Homeless People: A Black Perspective, CHAR, 1995 and Homelessness Amongst Young Black Minority Ethnic People in England, Race and Public Policy Unit, University of Leeds, 1996.
3. Homelessness Amongst Young Black Minority Ethnic People in England, Davies J and Lyle S with Deacon A, Law I, Julienne L and Kay H, Race and Public Policy Research Unit, University of Leeds, CHAR and the Federation of Black Housing organisations, January 1996.
4. Evidence submitted to the inquiry by Shelter Cymru.
5. St. Mungos press release and statistical analysis, May 1996.
6. Study of Homeless Applicants, O'Callaghan B and Dominion L with Evans A, Dix J, Smith R, Williams P and Zimmeck M, Department of the Environment, HMSO, 1996.
7. See for example Study of Homeless Applicants , Department of Environment 1996 and The New Picture of Youth Homelessness in Britain, Nassor IAA and Simms, Youth Affairs Briefing, Centrepoint, 1996.
8. The New Picture of Youth Homelessness in Britain, Nassor IAA and Simms A, Youth Affairs Briefing, Centrepoint, 1996.
9. Nowhere to Hide - Giving Young Runaways a Voice, Centrepoint and NSPCC, 1996.
10. Single Homeless People, Anderson I, Kemp P and Quilgars D, Department of the Environment, HMSO, 1993.
11. In 1994/95 single 16 to 25-year olds who were not pregnant accounted for 27% of all homeless applicants to local authorities in Northern Ireland and 25% in Scotland. Homelessness statistics for England and Wales do not include an age breakdown. However, a study of homeless applicants undertaken in nine local authorities in England in 1992/93 also found that 16 to 25-year olds (single, not pregnant) made up 23% of all applicants (Study of Homeless Applicants, 1996).
12. Evidence submitted to the inquiry.
13. Evidence submitted to the inquiry.
14. Evidence submitted to the inquiry.
15. Evidence submitted to the inquiry.
16. Leaving Home, Jones G, Open University Press 1995.
17. Evidence submitted to the inquiry.
18. Evidence submitted to the inquiry.

19. Evidence submitted to the inquiry.
20. Evidence submitted to the inquiry.
21. Evidence submitted to the inquiry.
22. Homelessness legislation is included in the Housing Act 1985 (part III) for England and Wales, the Housing (Scotland) Act 1987 (part II) for Scotland and the Housing (Northern Ireland) Order 1988 No (NI 23), for Northern Ireland. A new Housing Bill was passing through Parliament as this report went to press.
23. A survey by CHAR undertaken in 1993 found that only 23% of authorities accepted 16/17-year olds as vulnerable under the homelessness legislation on the basis of age alone (Conflicting Priorities - Homeless 16 and 17 Year Olds: A Changing Agenda for Housing Authorities?, Kay H. CHAR, 1994).
24. Since 1991 Department of the Environment homelessness (p1E) statistics have focussed on applicants who have been accepted for rehousing under the legislation rather than on those who have applied for assistance.
25. Single Homeless People, Anderson I, Kemp P, and Quilgars D, Department of the Environment, HMSO, 1993.
26. Advice Services for Single Homeless People in London, SHAC, Joseph Rowntree Foundation Housing Research Findings 127, 1994.
27. See, for example, Right to Care: Good Practice in Community Care Planning for Single Homeless People, Leigh C, CHAR, 1993 and Acting in Isolation: An evaluation of the effectiveness of the Children Act for young homeless people, McCluskey J, CHAR, 1994.
28. Single and Homeless in Hampshire, Baker L, with Watson L, and Allan G, University of Southampton, 1995.
29. Housing Demand and Need in England, 1991 to 2011, Holmans A, 1995.
30. Housing Need, Volume 1, Report together with the Proceedings of the Committee, Environment Committee, House of Commons Session 1995-96, HMSO, 1996.

PART 1
SECTION 2

1. Labour Force Survey statistics, 1994/95.
2. Never had it so good? The truth about being young in 90's Britain, British Youth Council, 1996.
3. Low Pay Unit Fact Sheet, 1996
4. Department of Employment, 1995.
5. Black Employment Institute
6. Claimant figures and so excludes most 16 and 17 year olds, Youthaid Working Brief, Issue 70, Dec. 1995/Jan 1996.
7. See, for example, Review of Qualifications for 16-19 Year Olds, Dearing R, March 1996; Tackling Long Term Unemployment, CBI, 1994
8. Basic Skills Agency 1996
9. See, for example, CBI (1994), British Chamber of Commerce (1994), Engineering Employers Federation and Engineering Council (1994).

10. School Leavers Destinations, UK Heads of Careers Services Association, in Taking Their Chances, Chatrik B and Maclagan I, Coalition on Young People and Social Security, Youthaid and the Children's Society.
11. Coalition on Young People and Social Security, briefing on young people and benefits, July 1995.
12. For example, Taking Their Chances; Education, Training and Employment Opportunities for Young People, Chatrik B and Maclagan I, Coalition on Young People and Social Security, Youthaid and The Children's Society; In Search of Work: CAB evidence on employment and training programmes for unemployed people, National Association of Citizens Advice Bureaux, 1994;
    A Broken Promise, Coalition on Young People and Social Security, Youthaid and The Children's Society, 1992;
    Review of Qualifications for 16-19 Year Olds, Dearing R, 1996.
13. Review of Qualifications for 16-19 Year Olds, Dearing R, 1996.
14. Tackling Long Term Unemployment, CBI, 1994
15. Disaffection and Non-Participation in Education, Training and Employment by Individuals Aged 18-20, Aspire Consultants (on behalf of TEC Chief Executives Network on Equal Opportunities and Special Training Needs), Department for Education and Employment, 1996.
16. Modest but Adequate; summary budgets for sixteen households, Family Budget Unit, 1995.
17. See for example, Severe Hardship; CAB evidence on young people and benefits, National Association of Citizens Advice Bureaux, 1992; Young People and Severe Hardship, Coalition on Young People and Social Security, 1991.
18. Taking Their Chances; Education and Employment Opportunities for Young People, Chatrik B and MaClagen I COYPSS, Youthaid and Children's Society, 1995; 1996 data provided by Youthaid.
19. For example, Severe Hardship; CAB evidence on young people and benefits, National Association of Citizens Advice Bureaux, 1992.
20. A Survey of 16 and 17 Year Old Applicants for Severe Hardship Payments, MORI, 1991.
21. Compared with someone claiming before 8th April 1996. There is transitional protection for those claiming between 8th April 1996 and 4th October 1996, Working Brief, April 1996.
22. For example, COYPSS, CHAR, NACAB.
23. Department of Social Security.
24. Department of Social Security in response to the Social Security Advisory Committee recommendations on the new Housing Benefit changes.
25. Leaving home and household formation by young men and women, Holmans A, in Housing in England 1994/95, Social Survey Division of Office of National Statistics on behalf of the Department of the Environment, HMSO, 1996.
26. See for example, The Bare Necessities: The Experience of Homeless People and the Discretionary Social Fund, CHAR, London Homeless Forum and Homeless Network, 1994
27. Eighth Report of the Social Security Advisory Committee.
28. New Earnings Surveys, HMSO, 1985 and 1995.
29. British Household Panel Survey.

30. For example, Mortgage Possession, Ford J, in Housing Studies, Vol 8. No. 4, 1993 and Single Adults: Affordable Housing and Housing Subsidies, Levison D and Randolph B, National Federation of Housing Associations, 1989.
31. Housing in England 1994/95, Social Survey Division of the Office of National Statistics on behalf of the Department of the Environment, HMSO, 1996.
32. Private Landlords and Housing Benefits, Centre for Housing Policy, University of York, 1996
33. Mortgage Possession, Ford J in Housing Studies, Vol 8. No. 4.
34. Housing Homeless People in the Private Rented Sector, Joseph Rowntree Foundation, Housing Research Finding 169, Centre for Housing Policy, University of York, 1996.
35. See, for example, Living in Temporary Accommodation: A Survey of Homeless People, Thomas A and Niner P, Department of the Environment, 1989; Alternatives to bed and breakfast Accommodation, Evans A, National Housing and Town Planning Council, 1991; Out of Sight: London's Continuing B+B Crisis, Carter M, South Bank University 1995; Wasting Money: Wasting Lives, Shelter, 1990.
36. For example, in 1987 there were 7,970 households in London who were in Bed and Breakfast hotels, having been placed there by local authorities. In March 1994 this figure had declined to 2,178.
37. Out of Sight: London's Continuing B+B Crisis, Carter M, South Bank University, 1995.
38. Halifax House Price Index, Fourth Quarter 1995.
39. The homelessness legislation is currently included in Housing Act 1985 (Part III) for England and Wales, the Housing (Scotland) Act 1987 part 11 for Scotland and the Housing (Northern Ireland) Order 1988 No (NI 23) for Northern Ireland. A new Housing Bill was passing through Parliament as this publication went to press.
40. National Statistics Office.
41. Housing Allocations: Report of a Survey of Local Authorities in England and Wales, Institute of Housing, 1990.
42. Housing and Construction Statistics.
43. CORE statistics, National Federation of Housing Associations.
44. Routes into Local Authority Housing: A study of local authority waiting lists and new tenancies, Prescott-Clarke P, Clemens S and Park A, Department of the Environment, HMSO, 1994.
45. See, for example, Acting in Isolation: An evaluation of the effectiveness of the Children Act for young homeless people, McCluskey J, CHAR 1994.
46. The Children Act and Youth Homelessness in Wales, Hoffman S, Shelter Cymru, 1995.
47. Homelessness Code of Guidance for Local Authorities (Third Edition), Department of the Environment, Department of Health, Welsh Office, HMSO, 1991.
48. Conflicting Priorities:homeless 16 and 17 year Olds: A changing agenda for housing authorities?, Kay H, CHAR, 1994.
49. For example, Right to Care: Good practice in community care planning for single homeless people, Leigh C, CHAR,1993, Strategic Planning for Vulnerable Single Homeless People: The Housing Association Role, Dix J and Evans A, Housing for Wales, 1996.

PART 1
SECTION 3

1. Household Formation and Tenure Decisions Among the 1958 Birth Cohort: A Descriptive Analysis, Di Salvo P, Ermisch J and Joshi H, National Child Development Study Working Paper 41, August 1995.
2. Leaving Home and Household Formation by Young Men and Women, Holmans A, in Housing in England 1994/95, Social Survey Division of the Office of National Statistics on behalf of the Department of the Environment, HMSO, 1996.
3. Pre-family lifestyles - Mintel 1996.
4. See, for example, Holmans A, 1996; Mintel, 1996; Ermisch J, Di Salvo P, Joshi H, 1996.
5. Deferred Citizenship; a coherent policy of exclusion?, Jones G, National Youth Agency Occasional Paper, March 1996.
6. Leaving Home, Jones G, Open University Press, 1995.
7. For example, a Centrepoint survey of young homeless people undertaken in 1996 found that 86% had been forced to leave home (The New Picture of Youth Homelessness in Britain, Nassor IAA and Simms A, Youth Affairs Briefing, Centrepoint, 1996).
8. The New Picture of Youth Homelessness in Britain, Nassor IAA and Simms A, Youth Affairs Briefing, Centrepoint, 1996.
9. Centrepoint annual statistics.
10. Four in Ten, Hendessi M, CHAR, 1992.
11. Submission to the Inquiry.
12. For example, G Jones (1993), Stockley and Bishopp (1993), Hutson and Liddiard (1991).
13. Department of Social Security, Households Below Average Income, a statistical analysis 1979-1992/93, and revised edition, HMSO, 1995.
14. Social Security Committee, second report, Low Income statistics:Low Income Families 1979-1989, HMSO, 1993; and Social Security Committee, First report, Low Income Statistics; Low Income Families, 1989-1992, HMSO, 1995.
15. Poverty is defined as below 50% of average income after housing costs. Department of Social Security, Households below Average Income; A statisical analysis, 1979-1988/89 and 1979-1992/93, and revised edition, 1992 and 1995.
16. Work out or Work in?: Contributions to the debate on the Future of Work, Meadows P. (Ed.), Joseph Rowntree Foundation, 1996.
17. See, for example, Poverty:The Facts, Oppenheim C and Harker L, Child Poverty Action Group, 1996.
18. Homes for our Children, National Housing Forum.
19. Household Formation and the Housing Tenure Decisions of Young People, Ermisch J, Di Salvo P. and Joshi H, Occasional paper 95-1, ESRC Research Centre on Micro-social Change, University of Essex, 1995.
20. 1981 and 1991 Census.
21. Leaving Home Jones G, Open University Press, 1995.
22. For example, Hutson and Liddiard (1991) and Stockley and Bishopp (1991).
23. The Relationship Between Family Life and Young People's Lifestyles, Joseph Rowntree Foundation, 1996.

24. Family Support for Young People, G Jones , Family Policy Studies Centre, 1995.
25. See for example, "Carefree and Homeless; Why so Many Careleavers are Homeless and will the Children Act Make a Difference?", Young Homeless Group, 1991, "A Lost Generation? A Survey of the Problems Faced by Vulnerable Young People Living on Their Own" National Children's Homes, 1993; Centrepoint Annual Statistics; Single Homeless People, Anderson I, Kemp P and Quilgars D, Department of the Environment, HMSO, 1993.
26. Household Formation and the Housing Tenure Decisions of Young People, Ermisch J. Di Salvo P and Joshi H, Occasional Paper 95-1, ESRC Research Centre on Micro-Social Change, University of Essex, 1995.
27. First Key has calculated that on average a child in care experiences 4 planned moves before they are 15 years old.
28. Moving On, Biehal N, Claydon, Stein and wade J, HMSO, 1995.
29. Leaving Care in the 1990s, Broad B, Aftercare Consortium, 1993.
30. Your're on Your Own, West A, Save the Children, 1995.
31 Prepared for Living, Leaving Care Research Project, Biehal N, Claydon J, Stein M and Wade J, University of Leeds, 1992.
32. Conflicting Priorities: Homelessness 16 and 17 year olds: A Changing Agenda for Housing Authorities?, H. Kay, CHAR, 1994.
33. Homeless Young Black and Minority Ethnic People in England, Davies J, Lyle S, with Deacon A, Law I, Julienne L and Kay H, Race and Public Policy Unit, University of Leicester, Federation of Black Housing Organisations, CHAR, 1996.
34. Planning for Action: The Children Act and Young Homeless people - A Black perspective, Federation of Black Housing Organisations and CHAR, 1995.
35. Study of Homeless Applicants, O'Callaghan B, and Dominion L with Evans A, Dix J, Smith R, Williams P, and Zimmeck M, Department of the Environment, HMSO, 1996.
36. Census statistics, Office of National Statistics.
37. The New Picture Of Youth Homelessness In Britain, Nasser I and Simms A, Youth Affairs Briefing, Centrepoint, 1996.
38. Dept. of Employment.
39. See, for example, "Sorry It's Gone": Testing for Racial Equality, Commission for Racial Equality, 1990 and Young, Black and Homeless in London, O'Mahoney B and Ferguson D, 1991.
40. The homelessness legislation is currently included in Housing Act 1985 (Part III) for England and Wales, the Housing (Scotland) Act 1987 part 11 for Scotland and the Housing (Northern Ireland) Order 1988 No (NI 23) for Northern Ireland. A new Housing Bill was passing through Parliament as this publication went to press.
41. The Social Security (persons from abroad) Misc. amendment regulations 1996.
42. For example, Poverty and Prejudice, Carter M, Commission for Racial Equality and the Refugee Council, 1996; Welcome to the UK: The Impact of the Removal of Benefits from Asylum Seekers, The Refugee Council.
43. For example, Poverty and Prejudice, Carter M, Commission for Racial Equality and the Refugee Council, 1996.

44. Single Homeless People, Anderson I, Kemp P, and Quilgars D, Department of the Environment, 1993.
45. Evidence submitted to the inquiry.

PART 1
SECTION 4

1. Single Homeless People, Anderson I, Kemp P, and Quilgars D, Department of the Environment, 1993.
2. Essex and Hertfordshire Homelessness Survey 1993, Hertfordshire Accommodation Project and the Single Homeless Project in Essex, 1993.
3. Evidence submitted to the Inquiry.
4. Evidence submitted to the Inquiry.
5. Evidence submitted to the Inquiry by the Foyer Federation.
6. Annual client statistics, Centrepoint.
7. See, for example, More Than Somewhere to Live: Housing's Impact on Healthy Communities, Robinson F, Spencer S, Wood M, and Keithley J, A report for the National Housing Forum sponsored by the Joseph Rowntree Foundation, 1996.
8. A Lost Generation? A survey of the Problems Faced by Vulnerable Young People Living on their Own, National Children's Homes, 1993.
9. Off to a Bad Start, The Mental Health Foundation, (forthcoming).
10. See for example, Surveys of Psychiatric Morbidity Among Homeless People, HMSO, 1996.
11. See, for example, Unhealthy Societies: The Affliction of Inequality, Routledge, 1996.
12. A survey of 505 drug misusing clients carried out in October 1994 as part of Turning Point's submission to the Task Force on the Misuse of Drugs.
13. Annual statistical returns from Turning Point's drug and alcohol projects for the period 1994/95.
14. Smoke and Whispers, Flemen K, Turning Point Hungerford Project.
15. Hearing Young People, Mattos C, CHAR (forthcoming).
16. Evidence submitted to the Inquiry.
17. Evidence submitted to the Inquiry.
18. Evidence submitted to the Inquiry.
19. Policy Statement, Scottish Drugs Forum.
20. Quoted in evidence of the links between homelessness and the Criminal Justice System, NACRO Occasional Paper, 1993.
21. Single Homeless People, Anderson I, Kemp P, Quilgars D, Department of the Environment, HMSO, 1993.
22. Evidence submitted to the Inquiry.
23. The Housing and Support Needs of Young Homeless People in Merthyr Tydfil, Hutson S et al, University of Wales Swansea, Occasional Paper 28, 1995.
24. Evidence submitted to the Inquiry.
25. Evidence submitted to the Inquiry.

PART 2

(referenced as one section)

1. Para 10.4, Homelessness Code of Guidance for Local Authorities (Third Edition), Department of the Environment, Department of Health, Welsh Office, HMSO, 1991.
2. Housing Act 1985, Part III.
3. Uncertain Futures: Interim report of a cohort study of young people rehoused in Newcastle upon Tyne, Keenan P. and McHanwell J, Newcastle City Council, submitted as evidence.
4. See, for example, Leaving Care and After, Garnet L, National Children's Bureau, 1992; Moving On, Stein M, Biehal N, Claydon J, Wade J, HMSO, 1995; Your'e on Your Own, West A, Save the Children, 1995.
5. See, for example, Leaving Institutions, Scottish Council for Single Homeless, 1996 and The Housing Needs of Ex-prisoners, Centre for Housing policy, University of York, 1996.
6. The Housing Needs of Ex-prisoners, Centre for Housing Policy, University of York, 1996.
7. Letting Housing Association Homes to Under Eighteen Year Olds: A Model Licence and Tenancy Agreement for Occupants Under the Age of Eighteen, The Welsh Federation of Housing Associations, 1994.
8. See, for example,Shared Accommodation in England 1990, Green H. and Holdroyd S, HMSO, 1992; Single Homeless People, Anderson I, Kemp P and Quilgars D, Department of the Environment, HMSO, 1993.
9. Furnished Accommodation for Single People, Holmes C and Shaw V, PEP, 1990.
10. Difficult to let Sheltered Housing, Tinker A, Wright F, and Zeilig H, HMSO, 1995.
11. The Government's Response on Housing Need, HMSO, 1996.
12. Evidence submitted by the Foyer Federation.
13. Foyers: A step in the right direction, Annabel Jackson Associates, Foyer Federation, 1996.
14. The Rough Sleepers' Initiative: An Evaluation, Randall G and Brown S, Department of the Environment, HMSO, 1993.
15. See for example, The Future of Work: Contributions to the debate, Joseph Rowntree Foundation, Social Policy Summary 7, 1996.
16. Survey by the Volunteer Centre UK, 1991; and Youth Matters, Centrepoint, June 1994.
17. Creating Local Jobs from Construction Expenditure, Joseph Rowntree Foundation, March 1995.
18. See for example, Housing Associations and non-housing activities, Centre for Housing Research and Urban Studies, University of Glasgow, 1995.
19. Taking their Chances: Education, Training and Employment Opportunities for Young People, Chatrik B. and Maclagan I, Coalition on Young people and Social Security, Youthaid and the Children's Society, 1995.
20. See, for example, from SEH-based estimates of eligibility, 74% of all private tenants entitled to Housing Benefit claimed it, but amongst single people aged between 20 and 29 years the proportion fell to 60% (Leaving home and household formation by young men and women, Holmans A, in Housing in England 1994/95, Department of the Environment, HMSO, 1996).
21. Evidence submitted by NACRO.

22. See, for example, Right to Care:Good practice in community care planning for single homeless people, Leigh C, CHAR, 1993 and Strategic Planning for Vulnerable Single Homeless People: The Housing Association Role, Dix J and Evans A, Housing for Wales, 1996.
23. See, for example, Responding to Homelessness: Local Authority Policy and Practice, Evans A, and Duncan S, Department of the Env. HMSO, 1988; Acting in Isolation, McKluskey, CHAR, 1994.
24. See, for example, Singled Out: Loal Authority Housng Policies for Single People, Venns, CHAR 1985. The New Homeless: The Crisis of Youth Homelessness and the Response of the Local Housng Authorities, Thornton R. SHAC, 1990
25. Interim findings of the study are contained in Uncertain Futures: Interim report of a cohort of young people rehoused in Newcastle upon Tyne, Keenan P. and McHanwell J, Newcastle City Council, 1996, submitted as evidence.
26. Where There's a Will: Implementing Local Strategies for Single Homeless People, McKluskey J, CHAR (forthcoming).
27. The Government's Response on Housing Need, HMSO, 1996.

SUMMARY OF MAIN REFERENCES

1. Anderson I (1994). *Access to Housing for Low Income Single People: A review of recent research and current policy issues,* Centre for Housing Policy, University of York.
2. Anderson I, Kemp P and Quilgars D (1993), *Single Homeless People,* Department of the Environment, HMSO.
3. Biehal N, Claydon J, Stein M and Wade J (1992), *Prepared for Living,* Leaving Care Research Project, University of Leeds.
4. British Youth Council. (1996), *Never had it so good? The truth about being young in 90's Britain.*
5. Chatrik B and Maclagan I (1995), *Taking Their Chances: Education, training and employment opportunities for young people,* Cooalition on Young People and Social Security, Youthaid and the Children's Society.
6. Davies J and Lyle S with Deacon A, Law I, Kay H and Julienne L (1996). *Homeless Young Black and Minority Ethnic People in England,* Race and Public Policy Unit, Working Paper 15, University of Leeds.
7. Diddlin J (1991), *Wherever I Lay My Hat: Young Women and Homelessness,* Shelter.
8. Ermisch J, Di Salvo P and Joshi H (1995). *Household Formation and the Housing tenure Decisions of Young People,* ESRC Research Centre on Micro-social Change, Occasional Paper 95-1, University of Essex.
9. Hoffman S (1996), *Against the Odds: Youth Homelessness* in Wales, Shelter Cymru.
10. Hutson S and Liddiard M (1994), *Youth Homelessness: The Construction of a Social Issue,* Macmillan.
11. Jones G (1995). *Family Support for Young People,* Family Policy Studies Centre and the Joseph Rowntree Foundation.
12. Jones G (1995). *Leaving Home,* Open University Press.
13. Kay H (1994). *Conflicting Priorities: Homeless 16 and 17 years olds - a changing agenda for housing authorities?,* CHAR and the Chartered Institute of Housing.
14. Leigh C (1994). *Everybody's Baby: Implementing Community Care for Single Homeless People,* CHAR.
15. McCluskey J (1994). *Acting in isolation: An evaluation of the effectiveness of the Children Act for young homeless people,* CHAR.
16. Nassor IAA and Simms A (1996), *The New Picture of Youth Homelessness in Britain,* Youth Affairs Briefing, Centrepoint.
17. National Children's Homes. (1993), *A Lost Generation? A Survey of the Problems Faced by Vulnerable Young People Living on their Own.*
18. National Housing Forum. (1992), *Homes for our Children.*
19. Pleace N (1995). *Housing Vulnerable Single Homeless People,* Centre for Housing Policy, University of York.
20. Randall G (1988), *No Way Home: Young Single People in Central London,* Centrepoint.
21. *Social Work Inspectorate, the Scottish Office (1995), Working with Young Homeless People, HMSO.*
22. Young Homelessness Group (1992), *Young Homelessness: A National Scandal.*

Appendix 1

ORGANISATIONS SUBMITTING EVIDENCE

NATIONAL VOLUNTARY ORGANISATIONS

Action Group for Irish Youth
Action on Aftercare
Alcohol Concern
Artswork, Young People at Risk Project
Barnardo's
British Youth Council
CAB Scotland
Cahag (Children Act Housing Action Group)
Centrepoint
CHAR
Charity Projects
Childline Cymru
Children's Rights Office
Childrens Society
Community SelfBuild Agency
Community Development Foundation
Community Service Volunteers
Council for the Homeless (Northern Ireland)
First Key, The National Leaving Care Advisory Service
Foyer Federation
MAYC - Youth Service of the Methodist Church
NACAB
NACRO
National Day Centres Project
National Youth Agency
National Children's Homes
National Association of YMCAs
National Consumer Council
NCH Action for Children, Scotland
Quaker Social Action
Refugee Council
Save the Children
Scottish Drugs Forum
Scottish Youth Housing Network
Shelter
Shelter Cymru
Shelter Scotland
The Church Army
The Young Builders Trust
Turning Point
Young Homeless Group
Youth Aid
Youth Access

OTHER NATIONAL ORGANISATIONS

Chartered Institute of Housing
Federation of Black Housing Organisations
Housing for Wales
National Federation of Housing Associations

LOCAL VOLUNTARY GROUPS

Ark Community Housing, Gloucestershire
Barnardos Strathclyde Homelessness Service
Barnardos, The Base, Tyne and Wear
Bexley Borough Churches Homelessness Project.
Borderline (working for homeless Scots in London)
Braintree Foyer
Bristol Cyrenians
Bromley Churches Housing Action Group
Bypass, Bolton Young People's Advice and Support Service
Centre 33, Cambridge Homeless Persons' Scheme
CHAS Kirklees
Chesterfield Young Persons' Project
City Centre Initiative, Glasgow

Community Campus, Cleveland
Consortium (voluntary agencies, South East London)
Coventry Cyrenians
Crouchfield Young Homeless Project
Dartford YMCA
Durham Young People's Centre Association
Earls Court YMCA
First Move, Newcastle upon Tyne
Friends, Families and Travellers Support Group
Guildford YMCA
Hampshire Youth Bureau
Hertfordshire Accommodation Project
Homeless Action, London
Homeless Action (Housing for single women in London)
Hove YMCA
HYUP (Hackney)
Lancaster Council of Churches Group
Leeds Nightstop
Lifechance Project, Oxford
Melton Young Singles Trust
Mendip YMCA
Merseyside Accommodation Project
New Horizon Youth Centre
NOAH, Kent
Point 26, Young People's Homelessness Group, York and Selby
Richmond YMCA, North Yorkshire
Single Homeless Project, Essex
South West Herts Young Homeless Group
South Shropshire Young Persons' Housing Project
Southend Centre for the Homeless
St Anne's, Leeds
St Mathew's Centre, Northampton
St Basil's, Birmingham
St Christopher's Fellowship
Streetwise Youth
Swansea Cyrennians
Taunton Association for the Homeless
Teesdale CAB
The Gateway Project, London
The Society of St Dismas
The Key House Project, Bradford and North Yorks.
The Home and Away Project, Brixton, London
TORCH Northampton
Young Homeless Project, Leamington Spa
Youth Advisory Service, Hereford

LOCAL AUTHORITIES

Bath City Council
Cardiff City Council
Dumbarton District Council
Falkirk District Council
Grampian Regional Council
Hampshire Social Services
Hastings Borough Council
Hereford and Worcester County Council
Leeds City Council
Lewisham Social Services
London Borough of Camden
London Borough of Richmond on Thames
Manchester City Council
Mid Glamorgan Probation Service
Newcastle City Council, Housing Department
Newcastle Welfare Rights Service, Social Services Dept.
North Hertfordshire District Council
Portsmouth City Council
Sheffield City Council
South Ribble Borough Council
South Glamorgan County Council
Southampton City Council
Stevenage Borough Council
Strathclyde Regional Council
Suffolk County Council

LOCAL HOUSING FORUMS

Bedfordshire Accommodation Forum
Berkshire Special Needs Housing Group
Cardiff Multi-Agency Working Group on Youth Homelessness
Croydon Special Needs Group - Under 18 Sub-group
Gloucestershire Forum for Young Single Homelessness
Havering Single Homeless Forum
Key to the Door Project, Oldham Housing Forum
London Homelessness Forum
South East London Consortium
St Albans Young Homeless Group
West Lancashire Homelessness Working Group

HOUSING ASSOCIATIONS

Accord Housing Management Ltd
Arlington House Housing Association
Cymdeithas Tai Eryri
Peabody Trust
Shaftesbury Housing
Stonewall Housing Association
Stonham Housing Association Ltd
YMCA Peterborough
YMCA Cambridge
Yorkshire Metropolitan Housing Association

ACADEMIC INSTITUTIONS

Centre for Local Policy Studies, Edge Hill University College
Centre for Health Economics, University of York
Centre for Educational Sociology, University of Edinburgh
Family Policy Studies Centre
Housing and Society Research Group, University of Newcastle
The School of Social Studies, University of Wales, Swansea

OTHERS

Accord Housing Management Ltd
Birmingham TEC
Bradford and District TEC
Diocese of Hereford
Hereford and Worcester TEC
Lincolnshire TEC
Pieda
Tyneside Careers
WESTEC

Appendix 2

ESTIMATING THE NATIONAL INCIDENCE OF YOUTH HOMELESSNESS

The starting point for the estimate is the most recent official statistics on the number of young people who applied as homeless to local authorities in England, Scotland, Wales and Northern Ireland. The proportion of young homeless people who do not apply as homeless (derived from a Department of the Environment survey of single homeless people[1]) is then applied, to get a figure for the total number of young people who are likely to have experienced homelessness during the period. **This method generates a total figure of around 246,000 young single people who were homeless in the UK during 1995.**

It should be noted that the calculation is more likely to under-estimate than over-estimate the incidence of youth homelessness. Applications from non-priority households, including young single people, are more likely to go unrecorded by local authorities than applications from priority households[2]. Also, other surveys have found that the proportion of young single people who do not apply as homeless (because they are unlikely to be eligible for help) is higher than the level found by the Department of the Environment survey[3]. A more detailed explanation of the method of calculation is given below.

BASIS FOR THE ESTIMATE

Unlike Scotland and Northern Ireland, homeless application figures for England and Wales are not broken down by age. In order to obtain a figure for the number of young people who applied as homeless in England and Wales, we have assumed that the group represents 23% of all applicants. This was the finding of a Department of the Environment study of homeless applicants undertaken in nine English local authorities during 1992/93[4]. This is in line with the proportions in Scotland and Northern Ireland - young single people (who were not pregnant) represented 25% of all homeless applicants in Scotland during 1994/95, and 27% in Northern Ireland during the same period.

Table A3 below shows that 85,441 young people applied as homeless to local authorities in England and Wales in 1995, and 12,912 young people applied to authorities in Scotland and Northern Ireland during 1994/95 (the most recent period that figures are available for). We have assumed that the number of young homeless applicants in Scotland and Northern Ireland will be roughly the same in 1995 as in 1994/95. The total number of young homeless applicants in the UK in 1995 was, therefore, 98,353.

A Department of the Environment survey of single homeless people who were sleeping rough or living in bed and breakfast hotels or hostels in 1991, found that only two-fifths of 16 to 25 year olds had applied as homeless to a local authority. If we assume that this proportion applies to young homeless people more generally, this means that around 245,880 young people were homeless in the UK during 1995.

YOUNG HOMELESS APPLICANTS, UK, 1994/95

Country	Period	Age	No. applicants	Basis/Source
England	1995	16-25	81,294	23% of all applicants (Department of the Environment)
Wales	1995	16-25	4,147	23% of all applicants (Welsh Office)
Scotland	1994/95	under 25	10,300	Scottish Office
Northern Ireland	1994/95	under 26	2,612	Northern Ireland Housing Executive

TOTAL YOUNG APPLICANTS = 98,353

FOOTNOTES

1 Single Homeless People, Anderson I, Kemp P, Quilgars D, Department of the Environment, HMSO, 1993.

2 For example, Study of Homeless Applicants, Department of the Environment, HMSO, 1996.

3 For example, Advice Services for Single Homeless People in London, SHAC, Joseph Rowntree Foundation Housing Research Findings 127, 1994.

4 See Note 2

Appendix 3

ESTIMATING THE COSTS AND BENEFITS OF REDUCING YOUTH HOMELESSNESS

A Study for the Inquiry into the Prevention of Youth Homelessness
By David Lewis and Penelope Rowlatt

INTRODUCTION

Cost-benefit analysis aims to identify, quantify, value and assess all of the costs and benefits associated with a particular action, no matter to whom they accrue. The valuation of the costs and benefits is usually done in financial terms to enable direct comparisons to be made. In principle, therefore, one would wish to place a financial valuation on the non-financial consequences of the action. In practice, however, such costs and benefits are often hard to quantify and end up being left as unquantified items, noted in the text accompanying such an analysis.

This note describes a highly simplified spread-sheet analysis of the costs and benefits of reducing youth homelessness. A simple model is constructed of the impact of potential homelessness on the financial flows associated with a young person who has no particular special needs. The model allows estimates to be made of the costs and benefits which accrue over a two year period depending on whether the person actually becomes homeless or whether support is provided. After outlining the main characteristics of the model we explain the meaning of the individual parameters included in the model and describe the rationale for each of the figures. There is a wide variation in the confidence we can attach to the values of these parameters.

The model assesses the situation of a young person at a point in life when they are forced to leave their family home. Two alternative scenarios are analysed. In the first, the young person does not become homeless; instead he or she obtains suitable accommodation financed through Housing Benefit. Based upon assumptions about the likelihood of employment being obtained, and the wage at which this is provided, the financial implications both to the government (taxpayers) and to society more generally (including the person concerned and the employer) are assessed.

The second scenario examines the situation in which a young person is unable to find suitable accommodation and is forced to sleep rough. The financial implications to society generally and to the government (taxpayers) are outlined. In this scenario we assume that after a period of one year, the young person returns to live with a member of their family which is likely to generate a conservative estimate of the costs of homelessness. In reality, other less favourable outcomes are possible, and an adjustment is made to the analysis to take account of this.

The model compares costs and benefits under the two scenarios. It does not include the cost of implementing a policy initiative that changes the balance between the two outcomes. If the relevant policy initiative is cost free, for example, it might consist merely of relaxing some constraint by which access to Housing Benefit for young people is rationed, comparison of the two scenarios will give an estimate of the costs and benefits involved. However, if a more active and costly policy initiative is envisaged, the additional costs need to be included in the analysis. The question would then be whether the cost-benefit difference between the two scenarios exceeded the cost of the policy.

SUPPORT SCENARIO

This section outlines the assumptions behind the "support" scenario of the model (see table of results attached). In this case a young person, at risk of becoming homeless, obtains accommodation which is financed by the government through the financial support given by Housing Benefit.

The additional administrative costs of ensuring the person is able to access the "support" are not included in this analysis, since no assumption is made about what form it should take. If this consisted simply of relaxing some constraint in the way in which Housing Benefit is currently implicitly rationed, then the analysis below will capture virtually the full costs of the policy. If more active intervention is considered necessary then this would need to be costed if the analysis were to provide a balanced estimate of the costs and benefits.

It is likely that the later the intervention to support the homeless person occurs, the greater will be the costs of supporting the person, since those who have been homeless for long periods are likely to have need of a higher level of support. So by excluding these costs, we may, in fact, be underestimating the benefits of reducing homelessness.

We assume that the person is unemployed initially, otherwise they would be significantly less likely to be homeless. While the person is unemployed the government will provide Income Support and Housing Benefit. This will be the case for each week that the person remains unemployed. Hence, a key parameter determining the costs incurred under this scenario is the likely length of the period of unemployment.

We start by outlining the weekly financial flows associated with employment and with unemployment. Knock-on effects of the increase in employment, in companies' profits and the effects on government finances are not considered.

WEEKLY COSTS WHILE UNEMPLOYED

While the person is unemployed the weekly costs to society, borne by the taxpayer, will be the sum of the Income Support and Housing Benefit they receive. Income Support for a young person is currently (1996) around £37 a week.

Housing Benefit is equal to the rent charged for renting a property which the DSS regards as appropriate. Hence it is not a fixed amount; Housing Benefit varies significantly by region. The most appropriate type of property to consider first when estimating the level of Housing Benefit for young people is the rent of furnished property. In 1994-95, the average rent on furnished property was £62 a week.[1] However, this is the average weekly rent on all available furnished properties, including large family homes. The properties considered reasonable by the DSS will inevitably be concentrated towards the lower end of the scale. In fact, from October 1996 reasonable benefit is to be assessed on the basis of a room in shared accommodation. Hence the average property rent needs to be reduced significantly if we are to obtain an estimate of the average level of Housing Benefit for young people. **In making our estimates we have used 50 per cent of this figure, or £31, as the estimated average Housing Benefit payment for young people.**

These data suggest the cost of supporting the person is £68 a week, borne by the taxpayer, throughout the period during which the young person remains unemployed.

WEEKLY BENEFITS WHILE EMPLOYED

Once the young person obtains employment, he or she begins to contribute to the wealth of the country, contributing taxes and making their own rent payments.[2] They will generate profits for their employer, and the government will benefit from employers' NI contributions and corporation tax payments.

In April 1995 average weekly earnings for full-time workers aged 16-18 were £115. For those aged 18-20 average earnings were £166 a week.[3] Hence we assume that the average wage at which employment might be obtained is £140. (Wages for 21-24 year olds were somewhat higher, but these will include jobs for which high qualifications are needed and many of the homeless would be precluded from such positions.)

We calculate that the average tax rate on this wage (including National Insurance) would be about 16 per cent, so the individual would contribute about £22 to the government. The individual could therefore be expected to earn a post-tax income of about £118. Compared to the income whilst unemployed of £68 there is an improvement of about £50 per week. They will be able to meet their own rent payments and subsistence needs rather than relying on Housing Benefit and Income Support and will still benefit from an additional weekly income of £50.

When the person is employed they also make a contribution to the profits of the business employing them. This constitutes a benefit to the firm involved and will also increase government revenues through corporation tax.

In 1994 industrial and commercial companies earned gross trading profits of £102,028 million.[4] Given an employed workforce of around 25 million, this is equivalent to about £80 per employee per week. Since this analysis is likely to be most concerned with relatively poorly paid and untrained workers we reduce this figure by 50 per cent, to £40 per week. We assume that 80 per cent of this profit remains with the firm, and 20 per cent is passed on to the government in corporation tax. National Insurance contributions by the employer (9 per cent) account for a further payment of £13 to the government.

UNEMPLOYMENT LIKELIHOOD AND DURATION

Data from Social Trends 1996 suggest that for someone aged 20-29, there is a 20 per cent probability that unemployment will last longer than two years. For our model, where we are assuming the young person is initially unemployed, we take that as implying that there is a 20 per cent probability that the young person who is unemployed and forced to leave their family home will not find employment during the two year period of the model.

We now consider the 80 per cent who would find work at some point during the two years. Amongst this group the average duration of unemployment would be 33 weeks. However, this does not imply that they will work for the full two year period except for 33 weeks, since they may also lose a job. To reflect this we assume that such a person spends 15 per cent[5] of the remaining time unemployed. Hence, on average, a person who finds work during the two year period will work for around 60 weeks.[6]

Thus, we assume that for a young person who has housing there is a 20% probability that they will not work over the two years and a 80% probability that they will work for 60 weeks out of the total 104 weeks.

CONCLUSION

These data suggest that if the individual is employed for 60 weeks of the two year period there might be a total net benefit to society of around £4,500, a benefit of £7,500 (£125 a week for 60 weeks) offset by a cost of £3,000 (£68 a week for 44 weeks). However, most of this benefit accrues to the employer and the individual concerned. The taxpayer faces a net cost of around £400, a cost of £3,000 while the person is unemployed (£68 per week for 44 weeks) offset by £2,600 when the person is employed (£43 a week for 60 weeks, made up of the employee's tax payment (income tax and National Insurance contributions), £22, the company's corporation tax payment, £8, and the NI contributions, £13).

If the person fails to find employment at any time during the 2 year period under consideration they cost society about £7,100 (£68 a week for 104 weeks), all of which would be borne by the taxpayer.

On average, given our assumed probabilities, there is a net benefit to society in this scenario of £2,200, but a net cost to the taxpayer of £1,700. However, the examination of how the results are arrived at in this scenario indicates how easy it would be to get different numbers with only a small variation in the assumptions.

HOMELESS SCENARIO

We now consider the alternative scenario; namely that the person becomes homeless. A number of strong assumptions are required to assess costs and benefits under this scenario. Some of the parameters should be regarded as estimates designed to convey the sense that homelessness imposes costs on both society and the government. For example, the fact that a homeless person does not receive Income Support payments does not obviate their need for food. A transfer of resources in some manner from the rest of society to the homeless person must occur in order for them to survive. Many of the figures used in this scenario should be regarded as ball-park estimates rather than accurate assessments. In many cases soundly based figures could only be established through detailed research.

We assume that the young person remains homeless for one year, after which they return to their family. The likely implications of other outcomes are briefly raised below. When the person returns home they are regarded as being in a less favourable position regarding employment as the individual who received Housing Benefit in the previous scenario (though they would not be eligible for Housing Benefit themselves). In other words, homelessness adversely affects the person's chance of becoming employed. We examine the implications of treating them as being equally likely to find work at the same salary in a sensitivity analysis.

WEEKLY COSTS WHILE HOMELESS

There are a number of ways in which the resources of the rest of society might be transferred to the homeless, fulfilling essentially the same function as Income Support in our other scenario. We assume that the homeless do not claim Income Support. Many may not be eligible, especially those aged 16 or 17, and others may not know that they are eligible. Some may be deterred by administrative hurdles which can be problematic if one has no address.

We make the ballpark assumption that from some source a homeless person receives an 'income ' of £37 per week; the same as Income Support which meets their basic subsistence needs, apart, of course, from housing. This 'income' could derive from a number of sources. Two possible means whereby resources may be transferred to the homeless from the rest of society are charity provision (begging or charities organised to help the homeless) and petty theft.

There are, however, costs of transferring these resources to the homeless, which basically represent a "deadweight loss" to society: charitable provision can be costly to organise, and the costs associated with petty theft are likely to be significantly in excess of the benefits obtained by those involved (stolen goods are generally sold at far less than their true value and there are costs to administrating insurance).

Further, given the vulnerable position of the homeless in society, there are costs associated with police action to protect them and to investigate crimes committed against them as well as the costs of investigating any crimes they may have committed. For example, if there were one crime associated with each homeless person every two weeks, if only one in ten of these is investigated by the police, and if the cost of investigating such a crime is £500,[7] then the cost of police work per homeless person would be £25 per week (before including a contribution to other aspects of law enforcement such as the judicial system, legal aid or the prison service).

COSTS OF HEALTH CARE

The rationale for increased health care costs is twofold. Firstly, even if other factors were equal, one would expect the homeless to have higher health care costs. Homelessness is likely to have an adverse effect on an individual's mental or physical health status, because, for example, of stress and anxiety, poor diet, or exposure. Furthermore, the homeless are likely to find it difficult to gain access to the primary health care system. If a medical condition develops further because of this, the cost of eventually treating it could increase. Alternatively the homeless may seek care in an accident and emergency department, rather than with a GP, which would raise the costs of providing health care.

It is difficult to quantify these effects. The suggested weekly figure of £7 equates to around £350 per year, and should be seen in the light of the fact that the annual cost of running the NHS is around £700 per person.[8]

RETURNING HOME

This part of the analysis uses the methodology applied to the previous scenario. The main difference is that, since the person stays at home (or with friends or relations), they do not receive Housing Benefit.

Since the remaining period of our analysis is one year the calculations of the expected length of unemployment differ. We calculate[9] that if having been homeless does not reduce the likelihood of an individual gaining employment the probability that the person will not work at all during the year is 37 per cent. If the person does work they would then do so for 29 weeks on average. However, it is likely that those who have been homeless will find it harder than others to find work quickly. To reflect this in our base case we halve the likelihood that the person gains employment to 32%. We also increase the expected unemployment duration of those who do work by 50% from 23 to 34 weeks. Alternative assumptions about these points are examined later in the paper.

SERIOUS EVENTS

Homelessness will increase the likelihood that a number of what we might term 'serious events' will affect a young person. These events, quite apart from generating large costs in human terms can also have large financial implications, and may extend over a lengthy period of time. These might perhaps include an increased risk of contracting a serious illness such as TB or Aids.

If homelessness caused crime and the young person were sentenced to a long prison term the financial implications for the public purse would be substantial. To imprison someone for one year costs the taxpayer in the region of £30,000.[10] The current social cost of someone being imprisoned for four years would exceed £100,000, even if discounted at an annual rate of 10 per cent.[11]

A (possibly small) proportion of young homeless people might 'drop-out' of society completely. In this case the costs of homelessness continue throughout the person's life instead of them contributing productively to society through employment. (On our assumptions employment gives a benefit of £125 a week. If homelessness continues, society will continue to incur costs, estimated in this analysis at £69 per week, roughly the same as the costs incurred if a person is unemployed and on

Housing Benefit. The difference represents a cost to society of over £10,000 per year for one person.) To reflect these various possibilities we assume that when a young person becomes homeless there is a 1 per cent probability that a serious event such as those above will befall them. We assume that these events have a current social cost (to taxpayers) of £100,000. It is impossible to attach much confidence to the accuracy of any such estimate. However, the resource consequences are certain to be significant and they should be considered. It appears plausible that the figures used underestimate rather than the overestimate the true costs.

CONCLUSION

If a person follows this scenario and becomes homeless for a year and then returns home the net costs to society (over the two year period we consider) depend on whether they find work in the following year or not. If they do not do so the net costs to society are estimated at about £5,500 (a total weekly cost when homeless of £69 over 52 weeks, plus the weekly Income Support of £37 a week for 52 weeks), including a net cost to the public purse of around £3,600 (the policing and health care costs of £25 and £7 a week for 52 weeks and the Income Support of £37 a week for 52 weeks).

If they do work the net costs are, on average, around £2,100 to the taxpayer (the same weekly cost of £32 for the 52 weeks of homelessness, with £37 Income Support for 34 weeks and £43 a week in tax and NI payment for the 18 weeks of assumed employment), and £2,600 to society (including the benefits to the individual and the company that employs him or her and costs incurred by society while the person is homeless).

Given the employment assumptions outlined above and a 1 per cent probability that a serious event (costing £100,000 lump sum) will occur these data imply that the average net costs to society are around £5,600 (a 32 per cent probability of a cost of £2,600 with a 67 per cent probability of a cost of £5,500 plus a 1 per cent probability of a cost of £100,000). The average net costs to taxpayers, on the same basis, are around £4,100.

COMPARISON OF ALTERNATIVE SCENARIOS

Comparison of the base case scenarios outlined above suggests that the costs, both to society overall and to the taxpayer are significantly lower in the "support" scenario where the person receives Housing Benefit and does not become homeless. Society benefits overall by around £2,200 during the two year period when the person initially receives Housing Benefit. If, instead, the person becomes homeless, there is a cost of about £5,600 over the period. **The net benefit to society of making Housing Benefit available to potentially homeless young people is therefore around £7,800.**

If the question is viewed solely from the taxpayer's perspective the difference is smaller. Costs to the taxpayer amount to about £1,700 over two years if the person receives Housing Benefit, and £4,100 otherwise, a saving of around £2,400. In other words, **this analysis suggests that providing Housing Benefit in this situation actually reduces costs to the taxpayer by over 50 per cent over a two year period.**

The net benefits to society exceed those to taxpayers as some benefits of providing Housing Benefit accrue to those other than the taxpayer. If a person finds employment it is not only the taxpayer who benefits; the individual and the firm who employs them both benefit directly. There could also be 'knock-on' effects although these are not considered in this analysis. Not all of the costs of homelessness are borne directly by the government; costs such as charitable provision and the part of the costs of crime are incurred by other elements of society.

ALTERNATIVE ASSUMPTIONS

It is interesting to examine how the above results alter when we change some of the key assumptions of the model. For example, one of the assumptions made when constructing the homelessness scenario was that having previously been homeless reduces an individual's chances of gaining employment within the following year. Consider two alternative assumptions about this:

- if we assume that homelessness has no impact on a person's subsequent chances of gaining employment then:
  - the net benefit to society of providing Housing Benefit to one person would be £5,800;
  - the net benefit to taxpayers would be £1,400;
- if we assume that having been homeless precludes a person obtaining employment in the following year then:
  - the net benefit to society of providing Housing Benefit to one person would be £8,700;
  - the net benefit to taxpayers would be £2,900.

Another assumption made was that a serious event, with an associated current social cost of £100,000 occurred with a probability of 1 per cent. Were we to assume that such serious events never occurred then all of the above 'net benefit' figures would need to be reduced by £1,000. It is worth noting that all remain positive. If the probability that such an event occurs was doubled the quoted net benefit figures would all rise by £1,000.

CONCLUSION

Our study concludes that, under plausible assumptions, the financial benefits of reducing youth homelessness outweigh the costs of doing so. The attached tables present the overall financial savings over the two year period, both to society and to taxpayers. This study has not attempted to estimate how many young people are in the exact situation considered in this model. Since the analysis only considers those who are at risk of being forced to sleep rough and have no particular needs other than housing the numbers to which it can be directly applied might be quite limited.

However, the point is clearly made. There can be considerable costs involved if young people, who are leaving their childhood home, cannot access the Housing Benefit needed to secure appropriate accommodation. Costs which in this analysis were markedly greater than the cost of intervention.

It should be emphasised that these conclusions are based upon a very tentative and simplified analysis. Only the initial direct effects are considered and many of the parameters on which the analysis is based result from reasoned intuition rather than being rigorously derived.

It should also be emphasised that this analysis has been restricted to financial costs and benefits. Human costs, such as the pain and suffering caused by homelessness, both to the homeless and to others involved, have not been evaluated.

ENDNOTES:

1. Social Trends, 1996 (page 182, Table 10.14).
2. Assuming that the salary they receive is sufficiently high. A poorly paid employee might remain eligible for housing benefit.
3. New Earnings Survey, 1995, Table AX4.2.
4. Economic Trends Annual Supplement, 1996, Table 1.12.
5. Is an (unweighted) average unemployment rate for 16-29 age group.
6. The estimates are in fact based upon the percentage of the unemployed, who have been unemployed for a given amount of time. They will represent accurate estimates of duration if unemployment is in equilibrium (constant.).
7. Operating the police force cost £7.7 billion in 1993 (Social Trends 1995, page 170). In 1993 recorded crime statistics show 57,000 robberies, 1.4 million burglaries and 2.7 million thefts (including handling stolen goods). In total, these account for around two thirds of recorded crime. We assume that these encompass a quarter of the police budget. This would suggest it costs an average of about £500 to investigate a crime of these types.
8. Although note that the average cost of providing health care will vary with significantly with age. Hence, the allowed figure could easily mean that the estimate regards homelessness as doubling the expenditure on health care on a young person.
9. Using the methodology of the previous section.
10. Calculated from Social Trends, 1995.
11. The concept of discounting takes account of the idea that future revenues are inherently less valuable than current ones. Discounting is ignored for simplicity in this analysis, since the period on which it focuses is relatively short. It would, however, be essential to discount at an appropriate rate in assessing costs which are spread over a long period of time.

SUPPORT SCENARIO

***(Costs and benefits over two year period)**

BACKGROUND DATA

WEEKLY COSTS WHILE UNEMPLOYED (IN £/WEEK)		
Housing benefit		31
Income support		37
Total weekly cost		**68**
Total weekly cost to taxpayer		**68**
WEEKLY BENEFITS WHILE EMPLOYED (IN £/WEEK)		
Weekly wage	140	
to government in tax		22
to individual (excess over £68 subsistence)		50
Employer profit from worker	40	
to government in tax		8
to firm		32
Employer NI Contribution		13
Total weekly benefit		**125**
Total weekly benefit to taxpayer		**43**
PARAMETERS		
Personal Tax rate	16%	
Employer NI rate	9%	
Corporation tax rate	20%	
Weeks unemployed (scenario 1)	44	
Probability of scenario 1	80%	

* First round effects only

ANALYSIS

SCENARIO ONE (Costs and benefits in £'000)
(Employed 60 weeks; unemployed 44 weeks)

Cost while unemployed	3.0	
Benefit while employed	7.5	
Net costs		**-4.6**
Cost to taxpayer while unemployed	3.0	
Benefit to taxpayer while employed	2.6	
Net costs to taxpayer		**0.4**

SCENARIO TWO (Costs and benefits in £'000)
(Unemployed 104 weeks)

Cost while unemployed	7.1	
Benefit while employed	0	
Net costs		**7.1**

AVERAGE NET COSTS (in £'000)
(Probability of scenario 1 equals 80%)

Average Net Benefit**	**2.2**
Average Net Costs to Taxpayer	**1.7**

** This benefit accrues to the young person and to the firm that employs him or her. The cost to the taxpayer is netted off.

NB: Costs and benefits to the taxpayer show the financial implications to the government. Costs and benefits to society include these but also include costs and benefits to the individual concerned, a firm who may employ them, and others directly affected.

HOMELESS SCENARIO

(Costs and benefits over two year period)*

BACKGROUND DATA

WEEKLY COSTS WHILE HOMELESS (IN £/WEEK)	
Income from various sources**	37
Increased policing costs	25
Increased health care cost	7
Total weekly cost	**69**
Total weekly cost to taxpayer	**32**

WEEKLY COSTS WHILE UNEMPLOYED (IN £/WEEK)	
Income support	37
Total weekly cost	**37**
Total weekly cost to taxpayer	**37**

WEEKLY BENEFITS WHILE EMPLOYED (IN £/WEEK)	
Total weekly benefits	**125**
Weekly benefits to taxpayer	**43**

PARAMETERS	
Weeks unemployed (scenario 1)	34
Probability of scenario 1	32%

* First round effects only

** For example charity provision or petty theft

ANALYSIS

SCENARIO ONE (Costs and benefits in £'000)
(Homeless 52 weeks; unemployed 34 weeks; employed 18 weeks)

Cost while homeless	3.6	
Cost while unemployed	1.3	
Benefit while employed	2.2	
Net costs		**2.6**
Cost to taxpayer while homeless	1.7	
Cost to taxpayer while unemployed	1.3	
Benefit to taxpayer while employed	0.8	
Net costs to taxpayer		**2.1**

SCENARIO TWO (Costs and benefits in £'000)
(Homeless 52 weeks; unemployed 52 weeks)

Cost while homeless	3.6	
Cost while unemployed	1.9	
Benefit while employed	0	
Net costs		**5.5**
Cost to taxpayer while homeless	1.7	
Cost to taxpayer while unemployed	1.9	
Benefit to taxpayer while employed	0	
Net costs to taxpayer		**3.6**

SERIOUS EVENT***
(Probability 1%) 100.00

AVERAGE NET COSTS (in £'000)
(Probability of scenario 1 equals 32%)

Average net costs	**5.6**
Average net costs to taxpayer	**4.1**

*** Such as serious illness or prolonged homelessness

NB: Costs and benefits to the taxpayer show the financial implications to the government. Costs and benefits to society include these but also include costs and benefits to the individual concerned, a firm who may employ them, and others directly affected.

Appendix 4

CASE STUDY CONTACT DETAILS

PREVENTION

Norfolk Peer Education Project - Beverley Knights, Centrepoint National Development Unit, Tel: 0171 629 2229.

Schools Education Scheme - Anne Oxley, Yorkshire and Metropolitan Housing Foundation, Tel: 0113 243 4621.

One-Stop Shop, the HUB Centre Bristol - Rob Risdale, Tel: 0117 909 6000

Dedicated Information leaflet - George Simpson, Rotherham Metropolitan Borough Council, Tel: 01709 382121

Out-reach advice, the City Centre Initiative, Glasgow - Carolyn Manson, Tel: 0141 227 6767.

A Through Care Strategy (formulated by the former Strathclyde Regional Council and carried out by Glasgow City Council),
Tam Baillie, Tel: 0141 287 8742.

Supported Lodgings Scheme, NACRO - Selina Corkery, NACRO Services Publications
and Information Officer, Tel: 0171 582 6500.

Rent Deposit Scheme, East London Homelink (Quaker Social Action) -
Mike Jenn, Tel: 0171 250 1193.

Nominated Tenancy Scheme, Derby City Council - Angelina Novakovic, Tel: 01332 255833.

Newcastle City Council Furniture Scheme - Paul Keenan, Housing Policy Officer, Tel: 0191 232 8520.

The Gateway Project, London - Mrs Lynda Stevens, Regional Housing Manager, Peabody Trust, Tel 0171 928 7811

The Richmond Foyer, North Yorkshire -
Carol Treweek, Richmond YMCA, 01748 824110.

Foundation Skills Training, Bristol Cyrenians - Jan Andrews, Skills and Learning Development Worker, Tel: 0117 955 0595.

Community Service Volunteers - Natasha Theobald, Marketing Unit, CSV, Tel: 0171 278 6601.

Off the Streets and into Work - Margy Knutson, CenTEC, 0171 314 0160.

Community Campus, Cleveland - Carl Ditchburn, Tel: 01642 247209.

North Tyneside Youth Self Build Scheme - Anna McGettigan, Community Selfbuild Agency, Tel:0171 415 7092.

The Home and Away Project , Lambeth - Myrtle Bernard, Tel: 0171 978 8267.

St Basil's Family Mediation Project, Birmingham - Geraldine Mulhern, Tel: 0121 2483.

RESPONDING TO HOMELESSNESS

The Young Homeless Project, Warwickshire - Tel: 01926 883179

Broad Horizons, Clackmannshire - Margaret Stewart, Project Manager, Tel: 01259 212044.

Hertfordshire Health Action Scheme - Joe Isaac, Crouchfield Young Homeless Project, Tel: 01727 833252

Moving-in Support, Cardiff Move-on Ltd - Richard Temple, Tel 01222 222262

Bypass, Bolton's Advice and Drop-in Centre for Young People - Peter Little, Tel: 01204 362228.

Artswork Young People at Risk Project -
Virginia Haworth, National Coordinator,
0171 936 3537.

LOCAL STRATEGIES

Centrepoint Oxfordshire - Beverley Knights,
Centrepoint National Development Unit,
Tel: 0171 629 2229

South Ribble - Gwen Crawford, South Ribble Borough Council, Tel: 01772 421491.

Appendix 5

SUMMARY OF 'COLLABORATING FOR SUCCESS: ORGANISATIONAL ISSUES FACING THE YOUTH HOMELESSNESS SECTOR'

INTRODUCTION

Two of the principal aims of the Inquiry into Preventing Youth Homelessness are to establish a consensus on the causes and scale of youth homelessness and to identify solutions to the problem that are innovative, effective and affordable. With these aims in mind, we have examined the 'supply side' of the youth homelessness sector - the many charities, government, local government and publicly funded agencies which offer services to the young homeless, concentrating on the organisational issues the sector faces.

The picture that emerges is one of a sector in flux, somewhat analogous to a young industry such as the personal computer industry in the 1980s or the multimedia industry today. Youth homelessness is a relatively new 'market' for charities and government agencies. It has arisen largely because steadily increasing competition for the state's welfare resources has squeezed young people on low incomes in housing need beyond the welfare umbrella. As in many emerging industries, this new 'customer need' has attracted a great number of players. They vary in almost every dimension, including their size, capabilities, structure, sources of funding, core activities, their scope and their co-ordination with each other. There is a very high rate of new organisation start-ups and failures. The new 'market' also attracts funds from both public and private sources. The sector players then compete for these resources to finance their particular projects. The evidence suggests these resources are not being spent as effectively as they could be.

In the business world, this would look like a sector ripe for rationalisation. We would expect a series of mergers, alliances and partnerships, as the organisations which delivered the best service to the young homeless at lowest cost emerged as the industry leaders. But in the absence of true market forces, how should this rationalisation occur? Having looked at some options, **we suggest that only if the organisations within the sector unite to manage the problem of youth homelessness in a co-ordinated fashion, area by area, will significant advances be made.**

Active local management of youth homelessness could take many forms, but any successful initiative would have to achieve four essential tasks:

- Develop a strategy based on an assessment of the varying needs of the different 'segments' of the homeless youth in each area.
- Get all the local agencies to agree to the strategy's targets, and to participate in its implementation.

- Implement the strategy according to a detailed action plan.
- Execute in parallel a co-ordinated fund-raising strategy.

This appendix summarises the thinking behind our recommendation and what its implementation might entail. It gives the conclusions we have drawn from the available data on youth homelessness.

The appendix falls into three sections. The first looks at how the young homeless are pushed beyond the welfare umbrella. The second section describes the nature of the 'youth homelessness sector' at present, suggests some reasons why it is having less impact than it might, and notes some more successful approaches. The final section describes how collaborative local initiatives could result in a more rational and effective allocation of the sector's resources.

YOUNG POOR IN HOUSING NEED ARE PUSHED BEYOND THE WELFARE UMBRELLA

Young, poor people in housing need become homeless because they must compete for scarce welfare resources with other claimants who are considered higher priority by the state. They are ostensibly covered by three types of welfare umbrella: by legislation and measures focused on all homeless people, by the Children Act, and by social security benefits. But they are not a priority category under the first, the second is ineffective or inadequately resourced, and the benefits they get under the third are too limited – and too complex – to allow them to buy desirable shelter in the private sector.

Young homeless people are not priorities for the usual housing welfare channels

Neither local authorities nor housing associations are able at present to treat young people in housing need as a priority.

Existing legislation does not give local authorities a duty to house young homeless people as a priority. They have been increasingly pushed beyond local authority housing provision by a rise in the number of households whom local authorities are legally obliged to treat as housing priorities. At the same time, the total stock of available local authority housing has been decreasing.

It is difficult for young homeless people to obtain housing association property since local authorities often nominate tenants for such accommodation. They are most likely to nominate their priority homeless.

As housing associations have been obliged to use more private finance, it has become harder for them to meet the requirements of private investors with schemes suitable and cheap enough for young, single people.

The Children Act is poorly resourced and implemented

The Children Act gives local authorities some responsibility for providing accommodation and support for homeless youth, but in practice other claimants on scarce local authority resources take priority. The Children Act states that *"Every local authority shall provide accommodation for any child in need in their area who has reached the age of 16 and whose welfare the authority considers is likely to be seriously prejudiced if they do not provide him with accommodation."* Where a young person has been accommodated, they are entitled to *"advice, assistance and befriending"* until they are 21.

However:

- Although homeless 16 and 17 year olds, care leavers in particular, may be covered under the Children Act, there is often no housing available for them.
- Social Services departments tend to concentrate their limited resources on younger children.

Young people on benefit have difficulty obtaining private sector housing

Those young people who qualify for Income s upport and Housing Benefit get little money. Benefit levels are set so that they can barely afford rents in the private sector. In any case, many affordable private rented housing units are taken up by local authorities, to house priority homeless. In addition, many landlords are unwilling to let property to tenants on benefit.

- Income support is £36.80 /week for 18-25 year olds compared to £46.50/week for people over 25. It has been technically abolished altogether for 16-17 year olds and replaced by a £28.00 severe hardship payment, with limited eligibility, or payments linked to training schemes.
- Housing benefit is supposed to be capped at an average market rate but in practice this appears to lag behind the market rate for accommodation suitable for young people.
- To house the growing numbers of priority homeless, local authorities have made increasing use of short-life leasing in the private sector. This has reduced the affordable private rental stock available to non-priority homeless.
- Landlords are often unwilling to let properties to young homeless people because of the complexity of Housing Benefit administration.

RESOURCES AVAILABLE FOR THE YOUNG HOMELESS ARE NOT ALWAYS SPENT EFFECTIVELY

Although the young on low incomes and in housing need tend to be pushed to the sidelines in housing allocation, there are some resources specially earmarked for them. But the homeless sector does not know enough about the precise needs of the young homeless in their area - their 'target market' - to formulate a coordinated and effective strategy for serving them. **If the players in the sector could work together to implement a jointly developed, needs-based, local strategy, it seems likely that they would be a more effective conduit for resources targeted at the young homeless.**

Some resources and services are available for the young homeless...

Funding for young homeless people comes from multiple public and private sources, and can be 'recycled' through several agencies. It is therefore difficult to calculate the total expenditure on youth homelessness accurately. But a crude estimate suggests that some £600 - £800 million is raised annually from central and local government and from voluntary agencies, with the majority coming from government sources. This is spent on Housing Benefit for 16 - 25 year olds (£487m in 1994/95), on housing association accommodation suitable for young single people and on grants made directly to youth homelessness projects.

The projects are executed by a variety of organisations who also raise money from voluntary sources. CHAR, the Housing Campaign for Single People, has 865 members included in the sector and there are over one thousand organisations nationally who provide some sort of service for the homeless. These organisations provide a mixture of services - accommodation, day centres, advice centres, schemes to help young people access private housing and homeless forums - policy-making and discussion groups for local agencies.

...But resources and services are neither co-ordinated nor matched to precise needs
Currently available resources appear to be having less than their potential impact for several reasons. There is no agreement among the players in the sector on the definition or size of the target group, nor on the segments within that group, and how to deal with them. Initiatives aimed at co-ordinating a response are still the exception, and their successes to date have been limited. Also the volatility of the sector itself makes co-ordinated, focused action difficult. The system may be diverting resources into too many projects which are too small to be sustained.

- **Problems in measuring needs.** It is difficult to measure the needs of young homeless people partly because the participants in the sector do not share a common definition of their target group. And however defined, the young homeless are hard to count. In addition, there is no agreed division of the category into 'customer segments' according to need, for example, into those with high support needs such as care leavers or substance abusers, and those capable of independent living.
- **Ineffective local strategies and co-ordination attempts.** There is evidence that agencies co-operate at an operational level, but there is no apparent co-ordination at the planning level. Projects are often opportunistic - they come about because a funding source or site suddenly becomes available so a project is quickly designed to make use of the money or building. Although many local authorities have developed homelessness strategies and established homelessness forums, their impact has largely been confined to improving information sharing between local agencies on the ground. They do not appear to have reduced homelessness substantially, or increased resources available to homeless people.
- **Volatility of the sector.** Since services are mostly provided ad hoc by local groups, they tend to come and go rapidly. This is partly because project grants are often 'tapered' over three years, to give the project organisers enough time to find more stable, alternative future funding. Many fail to do so, and disappear. There were 118 active charities providing accommodation to young people at the beginning of 1996, but 31% of these had started up since 1991 and 28 of those existing in 1991 had folded since then. The average size of the organisations which folded was half that of the successful organisations.

Coordinated efforts to tackle known needs are likely to be more successful
We would expect that the resources available to help young homeless people would achieve more impact if the sector was better organised to channel funds according to needs-based local strategies. Where this type of approach has already been tried – for example by the Centrepoint National Development Unit in Oxfordshire and in the American cities of St. Louis, Washington, New York and Houston – it appears to have had remarkable success.

These local initiatives have relied on a small core group to co-ordinate needs assessment, strategy, planning and fund-raising for a discrete locality (a county or a conurbation). They have found that there is often sufficient capacity in the existing operating organisations to deliver the required services to the homeless, provided the core group removes the barriers which prevent efficient service delivery. The most common barrier is an information shortage. The core group acts as a 'switching station' to match people in need with service providers, and to match the most effective service providers with resources.

- The Centrepoint National Development Unit has provided consultancy services to agencies outside London and piloted its own local scheme involving needs assessments and strategy formulation. They operated a project with considerable success in Oxfordshire and are engaged on projects in Warwickshire and Devon. The achievements of the Oxfordshire project included:
  * Raising £1.8 million in new funding
  * Developing 90 units of permanent social housing
  * Creating 4 access schemes
  * Creating 5 advice or drop in centres
  * Developing a foyer housing project
  * Conducting leaving home education in schools

ELEMENTS OF LOCAL MANAGEMENT TO PREVENT YOUTH HOMELESSNESS

The success of a local initiative would depend on the participation of all agencies in the area - statutory and voluntary. The boundaries of the area would depend on local housing pressure and the concentration of young homeless people. They would be likely to be based on cities or counties but not necessarily correspond to local authority areas.

The participating agencies would have to agree to act in accordance with a jointly developed local youth strategy. The participating agencies would together select a local core group from their members. The core group's first task would be to assess the needs of young homeless people in the locality, segment by segment. It would then formulate a local strategy to match those needs, and draw up detailed, linked action and funding plans to realise the strategy. The group would also be responsible for implementing the plans.

To ensure implementation, the core group would need to develop and maintain standard measurements of progress against plan targets. In addition, it would need to conduct periodic reviews of the strategy in the light of the results achieved.

The working paper and this summary were prepared for the inquiry by McKinsey & Company.